ATTITUDES OF ENTITLEMENT

Theoretical and Clinical Issues

The Virginia Psychoanalytic Society

Book Series: 1

ATTITUDES OF
ENTITLEMENT

Theoretical and Clinical Issues

EDITED BY

VAMIK D. VOLKAN AND

TERRY C. RODGERS

University Press of Virginia

CHARLOTTESVILLE

The University Press of Virginia

Copyright © 1988 by the Rector and Visitors
of the University of Virginia

First published 1988

LIBRARY OF CONGRESS
Library of Congress Cataloging-in-Publication Data
Attitudes of entitlement : theoretical and clinical issues / edited by
Vamık D. Volkan and Terry C. Rodgers.
    p. cm.—(The Virginia Psychoanalytic Society book series)
    Dedicated to the memory of George Kriegman.
    Includes bibliographies and indexes.
    ISBN 0-8139-1161-3
    1. Entitlement attitudes. 2. Psychology, Pathological.
    I. Volkan, Vamık D., 1932- . II. Rodgers, Terry C.
    III. Kriegman, George, 1917-82. IV. Series.
    [DNLM: 1. Attitude. 2. Human Rights. 3. Self Concept. BF 697
A885]
RC569.5.E48A88 1988
616.89—dc 19
DNLM/DLC
for Library of Congress   87-29579
                                                              CIP

Printed in the United States of America

Contents

Introduction to the Virginia Psychoanalytic Society Book Series

Vamık D. Volkan and
Terry C. Rodgers

Wıᴛʜ *Attitudes of Entitlement,* the first book of our series, we are honoring the memory of George Kriegman, M.D. (1917–1982). He was truly the founding father of psychoanalysis in Virginia. Upon graduating from the Washington Psychoanalytic Institute in 1951, he became the first privately practicing psychoanalyst in the Commonwealth of Virginia. He was a life-Fellow of the American Psychiatric Association and a member of the American Psychoanalytic Association and American Academy of Psychoanalysis. He was a decisive force in the establishment of psychoanalysis as an intellectual discipline and therapeutic modality in Virginia. One of his dreams was to establish a psycho-analytic society in the state which not only would bring Virginia psychoanalysts and psychoanalytically oriented psychiatrists to-gether but also would provide a focal point for the education and training of all who were concerned with mental and emotional suffering. Working with David Wilfred Abse, he cofounded the Virginia Psychoanalytic Society and served as its first president from 1976 to 1978. For the first four years of its existence and while it experienced growing pains, the society's monthly meet-ings were held in George Kriegman's home in Richmond. Mem-bers from various locations within the state came to the meetings, not only because they provided intellectual excitement and col-legiality but because of the warmth and cordiality of George and his wife, Lois, a clinical psychologist.

At the time of his death, George Kriegman was Clinical Pro-fessor of Psychiatry and Chairman of the Clinical Faculty Com-mittee of the Department of Psychiatry at the Medical College of Virginia in Richmond. In 1981 he was voted Outstanding Pro-fessor by the residents in psychiatry at the Medical College of Virginia. He was very proud of this and of his ability to teach.

Therefore, when the Virginia Psychoanalytic Society decided to undertake the intellectual endeavor of publishing a series of books, the members found it most fitting to dedicate this first volume to George's memory. This volume concerns a topic which was of great interest to Dr. Kriegman. He was for some time concerned with attitudes of entitlement, and his paper on this topic was published posthumously in the *Journal of the Amer-ican Academy of Psychoanalysis* in 1983. This paper is reprinted here with the permission of the *Journal*. It is followed by other essays dealing with the same and related issues by distinguished authors from Virginia and elsewhere in the United States and Canada.

The stated theme of this book may be viewed in a restricted or unrestricted sense. In the latter, it could be said to encompass, or at least be intimately related to, the whole of the human condition. From a more restricted developmental and clinical perspective, it covers the life span and all gradations of adaptation from the grossly pathological to the normal. Furthermore, the normal and pathological manifestations of entitlement attitudes are blended and interwoven at any cross section of the life cycle, and when viewed developmentally, what are normal attitudes at one phase of development may be abnormal at another. The shadings of attitudes of entitlement (or nonentitlement) are structured ego functions and, as character traits, relate to the whole of an individual's functioning. People with pathological entitlement attitudes are especially prone to projection of their conflicts into all their interpersonal relationships, thus creating a projective-introjective cycle in which the *other* participates in varying degrees. This interaction of "two selves" serves to maintain or alter the nuclear configurations of self and object representations that give direction to a person's character. The clinical and literary vignettes in the various chapters amply illustrate this phenomenon. While all the contributors to this first book are psychiatrists and psychoanalysts, the scope of the presentation of their ideas is beyond purely clinical issues.

Psychoanalysis, as a term, is applied to an agglomerate of theories for understanding the human mind, to a very specific treatment modality, and to a research tool to study functions of the mind. Here, in preparing this series of books, we are especially interested in psychoanalysis when it is a window between clinical (medical) issues on the one hand and general human issues such as psychological, social, legal questions or as an aesthetics and literature on the other hand. For example, in later volumes we expect to treat such topics as the relationship between depression, a clinical issue, and creativity, a general human issue, and the relationship between an individual's masochism and sadism which we see in our practice and political aspects of groups in conflict. In bringing this series to fruition, we plan to be interdisciplinary, not only asking practicing psychoanalysts to discuss development, normality, and the human issues as they are understood from the side of human psychopathology but having experts in literature, anthropology, sociology, and legal matters address the psychoanalysts. The phenomenon of entitlement is a final common pathway that derives from early deprivation, physical illness, altruism, aging, and so on and is related to narcissistic or depressive disorders. It is intimately related to the vicissitudes of narcissism. As such, it may be healthy or pathological, exaggerated or underdeveloped, but in all instances it reflects an individual's view of himself vis-à-vis his world.

Narcissism in its varied manifestations can justifiably claim to have been the preeminent focus of psychoanalytic clinical and theoretical interest during the past two decades. Even a cursory review of the extensive literature of this period is beyond the scope of this introduction. However, lest we lose sight of the ubiquitous and multifarious nature of narcissism, it is well to recall some seminal remarks of the prenarcissism phase of psychoanalysis.

Freud (1914) refers to narcissism as the "libidinal compliment to the egoism of the instinct of self-preservation, a measure of which may justifiably be attributed to every living creature" (73–74). Greenacre (1952) states, "From a biological viewpoint, narcissism may be defined as the libidinal component of *growth* which may, however, become turned one way or another by the vicissitudes of experience at *any time* in the course of life" (21, italics added). She further states:

> It is . . . the great enigma of life, playing some part at one and the same time or in alternating phases in the drag of inertia and in the drive to the utmost ambition, and contributing its share to the regulating function of the conscience. . . . narcissism is coincident with life throughout and . . . narcissistic libido is, in fact, to be found wherever there is a spark of life. It seems . . . evident that an increased early infantile anxiety can be expected to be associated

with a complementary increase in infantile narcissism; that, in fact, excess narcissism develops as part of the organism's overcoming of the excess anxiety before it can function even slightly as an independent unit in the environment. [47–48]

The above statements seem to extend the maxim that self-preservation is the first law of nature to include the psychic as well as the physical being.

We wish to thank all the members of the Virginia Psychoanalytic Society for their support for this project.

REFERENCES

Freud, S. 1914. On narcissism: An introduction. In *Standard edition*, 14:67–102. London: Hogarth Press, 1957.

Greenacre, P. 1952. *Trauma, growth, and personality.* New York: W. W. Norton.

ATTITUDES OF ENTITLEMENT

Theoretical and Clinical Issues

I.

Entitlement Attitudes:

Psychological and

Therapeutic Implications

George Kriegman

THE WORD *entitlement* is heard more and more often these days. The concept it refers to was honored by the Declaration of Independence: "We hold these truths to be self-evident, that all men are created equal, that they are endowed by their Creator with certain unalienable Rights, that among these are life, liberty and the pursuit of happiness," and the Social Security Act of 1935 expanded the idea in ways not dreamed of by the Founding Fathers. Since then it has been broadened still further by militant efforts to ensure the civil rights of various racial and social minorities within our society, and even applied to ecological issues on

Reprinted by permission from: 1983 *Journal of the American Academy of Psychoanalysis* 11:265–81.

behalf of the right of all living things to a biologically healthful environment. In psychiatry, we must deal with the right of the patient to refuse medication as well as with his right to treatment. Indeed, in most areas of modern life claims to entitlement made on political, social, religious, and philosophical grounds must be taken into consideration. In some circumstances it becomes difficult to separate matters of legitimate entitlement from those better called rising expectations. (It is important to differentiate entitlements that a person has a right to and the person's aspirations to be entitled.)

Obviously, the individual is significantly affected psychologically by the fulfillment or nonfulfillment of what he considers his entitlements. My private psychiatric practice has shown me, moreover, the importance of learning what an individual feels his entitlements to be, since while some patients may have unrealistically grandiose expectations of their entitlements, there are those, not necessarily different in circumstances, who do not feel entitled to say or do what others consider themselves entitled to do or say, who cannot assume for themselves the basic right of being human.

Chester M. Pierce, Professor of Education and Psychiatry at Harvard, published a paper (1978) on entitlement dysfunctions in which he stated that "entitlement dysfunctions are conflicts, real or imagined, microscopic or macroscopic, in which interpersonal confrontations about prestige/status are more salient and expressive than frustrations or obstacles over sex, dependency or aggression. In fact, prestige confrontations lead to trouble in these areas. The basic characteristics . . . are perceptual differences . . . in regards to rights, duties, privileges or obligations." He noted further that "ordinarily the issue involves a perception of the disrespectful and undignified use, misuse or abuse of someone's time and space." He postulated that "if one has too many, too fragmented or too intense entitlement disasters, there will be presentations of physical and mental symptomatology subsequent to feelings of fear, anger or envy." Pierce is focusing here primarily on the sociopolitical aspects of entitlement with their psychological ramifications.

Any number of examples of the disrespect for and the misuse and abuse of a human being's time and space could be cited. The fifty-two hostages in Iran provided us with an excellent example. And the widely publicized abuse of children and the elderly by parents and other relatives, as well as the widely recognized historical, economic, social, and educational discrimination against blacks, indicates the violation of the space, time, and rights of human beings. As students of human behavior, we are sensitive to subtle as well as obvious psychological effects to be expected from such violation. As society addresses itself to the question of human rights, sometimes with more attention to rhetoric than to precise definition of what is at issue, it behooves us to examine and evaluate the specific interpersonal and intrapsychic factors involved in the maintenance of "human dignity" and the appropriate honoring of "entitlement."

Many questions need to be answered. Are attitudes of entitlement primarily the result of sociological and economical disadvantage? Do persons who are sociologically and economically advantaged manifest problems in the area of entitlement? Do these attitudes of entitlement affect the individual's identity and self system? Why does one person bring suit for substantial satisfaction at a loss of a job, claiming sex, age, religious, or minority discrimination, when another person in comparative circumstances just accepts the situation? Above all, how can we account for the dramatic rise of those who find severe hardship in early life no deterrent to notable success? These are but a few of the questions involved.

I have found in my private practice a diversified group of patients who ran into stalemate in their treatment, or seemed unable to grow and develop in certain areas of their life, in spite of the considerable therapeutic progress they manifested in their attitudes and behavior. When I analyzed what impeded them, it became evident that these patients did not feel they were entitled to say or to do anything with the freedom others take for granted as a right. It was as though, having no basic rights, they constantly had to justify their existence. For example, such people often find it extremely difficult to express any opinion that offers disagreement with another's. When asked why they did not simply express themselves, they would say, "I didn't feel I could," or "Who am I to say anything?" or "What right have I to disagree?" In the case of several patients, these attitudes reached the point of absurdity; they maintained they had "no right to be wrong." To most of us, to be wrong is simply to make a mistake that we need to acknowledge and learn from in order not to repeat our error. But to the patients in question, to be wrong is sinful, a transgression that raises the question of their right to exist. It was clearly evident that no further progress could be made in altering the life-style of these patients as long as they doubted that they had any basic rights as human beings.

As I began to realize the pervasive nature of these attitudes of entitlement or nonentitlement, it struck me that this phenomenon was not limited to these particular patients. The same feelings must be experienced by those who have in reality always been socially and economically disadvantaged, and a deeper understanding of the psychodynamics of attitudes of entitlement might help us understand how life appears to them. This interest led me to search the psychiatric literature for material on the subject.

The first use of the word *entitlement* in the psychiatric literature appeared in Horney's book *Neurosis and Human Growth* (1950). In the second chapter, titled "Neurotic Claims," she discusses in considerable detail patients who expect to be treated in a special and sometimes fantasy manner and feel that this is their just entitlement. This is their neurotic claim. Horney, however, confines her discussion solely to this type of entitlement, which at present we associate with narcissistic personality disorders, and does not recognize other psychological aspects of attitudes of entitlement.[1] It was not until 1964 in an article by Murray on "Narcissism and the ego ideal" that the word *entitlement* again was used. This dealt primarily with patients convinced that they were uniquely entitled to have their desires accommodated. Freud, of course, dealt with the same type of narcissistic patients in his 1916 discussion of "Some Character Types Met within Psychoanalytic Work," and Jacobson made similar observations in 1959 in a paper called "The Exceptions: An Elaboration of Freud's Character Study," which appeared in *The Psychoanalytic Study of the Child*. But it was not until 1970 that the first definitive article on the subject, written by Levin, appeared in the *Bulletin* of the Philadelphia Association for Psychoanalysis. I could find only four subsequent papers on the issue: Solomon and Leven expanded on Levin's work in a paper in *Psychotherapy, Theory, Research, and Practice* on "Entitlement" in 1975; in 1977 Rothstein published "The Ego Attitude of Entitlement" in the *International Review of Psychoanalysis*, writing there only of narcissistic types of entitlement; *The Diagnostic and Statistical Manual of Mental Disorders* (*DSM* III) (1980) refers to entitlement as a diagnostic criterion for narcissistic personality disorder; and in 1978 Pierce wrote the paper already referred to dealing with sociological aspects of entitlement. Obviously, sociologists, social workers, economists, political scientists, and others have considered this issue, but their writings are beyond the scope of this chapter.

In this discussion of the literature I will confine myself to the paper by Levin and its elaboration by Solomon and Leven. Levin wrote of three groups of entitlement attitudes: (1) attitudes of normal entitlement; (2) attitudes of excessive entitlement; and (3) attitudes of restricted entitlement. He also pointed out that one may find "in many patients ... attitudes of both excessive and restricted entitlement."

1. The author is indebted to Morton B. Cantor, M.D., for bringing Horney's early writings on entitlement to his attention.

5

Attitudes of normal entitlement are the individual's expectation of having time and space to pursue and obtain appropriate satisfactions in life; they involve his right to do certain things and to expect others to do certain things. That is, he has the right to food, shelter, protection, etc., expects others to respect these rights, and is entitled to be righteously indignant if they do not. Levin points out that these rights are "highly specific" and involve not only specific satisfactions but also "specific aims." For example, every family member expects that the others will come to his rescue if he is threatened or challenged by an outsider—"We Joneses stick together." In the larger social unit, this attitude anticipates that doctors will come to the defense of another doctor, and that all Americans will defend their country if it is attacked—"America, right or wrong."

In a healthy family a child develops the attitude that he has certain rights to satisfactions that are appropriate to his age and level of development. His attitudes of entitlement are important to his sense of identity and his self-esteem. Such simple conclusions as those involved in a child's statement that "I am five years old and so I have a right to cross the street and play with my friends" or "Now I can stay up till nine o'clock and see 'All in the Family' on the TV" show how attitudes of entitlement contribute to the child's sense of identity and impart the basis of healthy self-regard.

Attitudes of excessive entitlement, however, involve exaggerated ideas of what the person has a right to do. People who have such attitudes seem to say, "The world owes me a living. I should always be approved of. I can do anything I want. I can have anything I want. My desires and needs are the most important thing in life. I should be catered to." They may make it plain that they consider themselves outstandingly charming and good-looking. It is usual to label such people arrogant, smug, selfish, demanding, pretentious, self-righteous, megalomanic, and, of course, narcissistic. They are often not aware of the adverse attitudes their behavior evokes in others; if they are, such negative reactions puzzle them because they do not realize their ego-syntonic belief in their own superiority is reality-dystonic. Levin notes also that "an attitude of excessive entitlement may be camouflaged by an overt posture of humility," in which case it is less likely to attract criticism or, indeed, be recognized by others for what it is.

These attitudes of excessive entitlement are fairly familiar to the psychiatric community because narcissism has long been a subject of research, beginning in 1914 with Freud, and continuing with the work of Kohut, Kernberg, and others. According to Rothstein, these attitudes are defensive, and developmentally evolved primarily from the mother's treatment of her child as a narcissistic object to gratify her own needs. Freud identified another factor that may account for an attitude of excessive entitlement; an individual may feel entitled to special privileges because of his having been an innocent victim of suffering in childhood. Solomon and Leven postulate two types of parents responsible for encouraging this attitude: self-righteous ones who rigidly assert that they always know what is best for their child and the uncertain, doubt-ridden ones whose children become stubborn in their conviction because of reaction formation to the vacillations of their parents.

I feel that attitudes of restricted entitlement or nonentitlement have not been sufficiently recognized by clinicians as factors in psychopathology, nor has their connection with social and economic limitations been duly acknowledged. Attitudes of nonentitlement involve the conclusion, "Who am I to want, desire, or expect anything?" Such a person is inhibited, feels worthless, inadequate, and defective, and virtually questions his right to exist. In some cases, his life can be justified only by the approval and acceptance given by a significant other. He feels that if he is the perfect good child, he then has a right to exist and perhaps be entitled to some satisfaction in living—providing, of course, he continues to be good.

7

Obviously, such individuals have a limited sense of identity. Levin notes that "such restrictions usually start in early life and may be based in part upon excessive shame or excessive fears of injury, including the fear of castration." He cites a case of Lichtenstein's in which the mother had excessively shamed her daughter and four cases of Hart's involving people "whose mother's excessive narcissism interfered with the son's identification with the father." As is true of attitudes of excessive self-entitlement, attitudes of nonentitlement or great limitation tend to be egosyntonic and thus accepted as indicating the way life is. It is not unusual for a patient with this affliction to say when it is brought to his attention, "Doesn't everyone feel this way?" and at times to defend strongly the attitude of nonentitlement by such statements as, "Everyone wants to be approved of; you have to do something to be someone." Frequently these patients will view what others consider their just rights as evidence of arrogance, selfishness, unfeeling, or imperviousness. "These individuals have a basically negative sense of identity, an unconscious sense of utter worthlessness," although, as Levin points out, "an attitude of restricted entitlement may be hidden by counterphobic mechanisms."

The development origin of attitudes of nonentitlement may be childhood identification with a parental figure with such attitudes, or the very early empathic perception that something in the relation with the mothering one was missing. Recent research by pediatricians, child psychiatrists, developmental psychologists, and geneticists clearly indicates that the newborn is biologically pre-programmed to respond to the mother. If, for whatever reason, the mother is unable to respond fully and appropriately in a nurturant manner, her newborn child will emphatically sense her failure and response in his behavior. We also know from Mahler and others that there is a normal symbiotic stage of development, and that any disturbance in this symbiotic stage will have a profound effect on the infant's development. Attitudes of nonentitlement do not indicate that the child was blatantly rejected but suggest that the mother may have conveyed to it some subtle unconscious dissatisfaction through a less than wholehearted tenderness that awakened in her child a sense of discomfort and a degree of dysphoric mood. The sensation of "something is wrong" is unconsciously translated as "something is wrong with me" because at that early stage of development the referential system is self-directed. The child who concludes, however unconsciously, that "something is wrong with me" experiences an underlying sense of shame and guilt. One who feels ashamed feels the need to atone for whatever it was that was shameful, and the result is the feeling of nonentitlement, the need to do something to compensate for the misdeed or failing. Thus people with this kind of early experience feel that they must be good, must behave in a fashion that will bring them approval and acceptance. Their concept of their worth and the justification for their living was always contingent on doing what they felt or assumed would be accepted and approved of by significant others. Thus they do not feel that they have any basic rights as human beings.

As patients such people must not be confused with masochistic patients who have a strong need to suffer; they do not have the need to suffer, and they gain no sense of satisfaction from suffering, although they may experience depression since many of their emotional needs and aspirations will not be fulfilled. Solomon and Leven point out that "masochistic patients may feel that they are entitled to pain; for it gives them a sense of self."

At this point I would like to expand, modify, redefine, and integrate this subject of attitudes of entitlement, some form of which I attribute to all human beings. I find Levin's classification of normal entitlement satisfactory, but I think it operationally more appropriate to call what he called "excessive entitlement" exaggerated entitlement. And I would call Levin's "restricted attitudes" those of nonentitlement. My clinical observation leads me to postulate that all human beings manifest all three types of attitudes in varying degree. The rationale for modifying Levin's classification is that "excessive" entitlement implies that the person has more entitlement than others, a quantitative concept. As I view entitlement, all persons have equal degrees of entitlement. Some people have unrealistically "exaggerated" their entitlement and have exaggerated expectations of how others should respond to their wishes. In those individuals whom Levin refers to as having "restricted attitudes," I feel a more appropriate term is nonentitlement attitudes because it is not a question so much of restriction, which also has quantitative implications, but of the person questioning his right to any entitlement whatever.

I would hold such manifestations minor when the exaggerated or nonentitlement attitudes are circumscribed and limited to specific situations. Everyone has some foible regarding his personal habits, for example, the honoring of which he feels entitled to. Some people feel fully entitled to be righteously indignant if the morning ritual of a cup of coffee and a glance at the newspaper is not allowed before any recognition of others in the household is required. Likewise, most of us allow ourselves to be bullied in some situations; the TV ad about the man cringing silently when taunted by the unfeeling man who has noticed his slipping dentures makes the implication, with which nobody seems shocked, that anyone in so awkward a situation has no redress. These minor manifestations do not, however, basically involve the sense of identity.

Attitudes of exaggerated entitlement or nonentitlement can, however, be a major factor in the individual's orientation toward life, a determinant of his sense of identity, and thus of his sense of worth, and result in psychopathology. Exaggerated attitudes are manifested clearly in pathological narcissistic disorder and in borderline personality organization. Nonentitlement attitudes are evident in characteriological disorders, schizophrenic conditions, and in many cases of depression. In either group, cognitive functioning is constricted in varying degree; anger, affection, guilt, self-assertion are warped. The result is that the person's sense and type of identity are distorted in one way or another, and as Harry Stack Sullivan once put it, he "is an inferior caricature of what he might have been." In addition, both these attitudes may involve only specific aspects and levels of the person's life. Occupationally the individual may manifest normal entitlement attitudes but in social or personal aspects of his life may have exaggerated or non-entitlement attitudes. For example, if the person has undertaken training in a particular occupation and been judged by the appropriate authorities to be capable, then he feels he is entitled to operate independently in that sphere; but on a personal level, since he was not issued a certificate, he has no independent rights. At one level, the person may feel he has the right to take the initiative but at the same time may not feel entitled to make a request which is seen as an imposition on someone. In turn, requests made to him are perceived as demands which he resents but feels he is obligated to fulfill. A person may have exaggerated ideas of what satisfactions he is entitled to but not feel he has the right to implement what would give him pleasure and gratification or feel that he is entitled only if he meets some prerequisites first.

My third postulate is that the etiology of attitudes of entitlement is bimodal: social and psychological. It is social inasmuch as the particular culture in which the person develops and lives predicates and imposes certain attitudes of entitlement. The WASP individual from an affluent family is likely to have more of a sense of normal entitlement, and probably varying degrees of exaggerated attitudes about it. On the other hand, a member of a minority ethnic or religious group who comes from a impoverished background will have less sense of normal entitlement and more sense of nonentitlement.

The social milieu into which a person is born, and in which he develops and grows, has less psychological effect on his sense of entitlement, however, than the interpersonal atmosphere of his childhood home, and the interlacing of social and psychological factors will determine the degree of normality or psychopathology he will manifest.

To illustrate this bimodal etiology of entitlement attitudes, I offer two short vignettes. The first case is that of a woman in her thirties from a wealthy WASP family. She was the third of four children, having an older brother and sister and a sister two years her junior. She had been considered an unusually enchanting infant and had been adored by her grandfather, father, and older siblings; but her mother, a cold and distant woman, disapproved of the family's doting on the child, fearing that such adulation would spoil her. The birth of the younger sister when she was two further diminished the attention she received from her mother, who turned her over then to the care of a stern and tight-lipped governess. During the next two years her grandfather died, her father was less and less at home because of increased business responsibilities, and her older sister was the only survivor of her original circle of adorers at hand. Nonetheless, she was an extremely well-coordinated, agile, and athletic child and her family thought of her as being able to do well anything she might undertake. She became, in effect, an "all-American girl," a princess of whom this "royal family" might well be proud.

Her early experiences had led her to develop exaggerated attitudes of entitlement; she expected that everyone would excitedly welcome her when she entered a room, and when they did not, she felt hurt and righteously indignant. As a dethroned little girl, she entered the oedipal period with an intense longing for the lofty position she had once enjoyed and followed the characteristic pattern of children in this period of development by urgently seeking attention from her father. He gave it to her readily enough when he was available, but she could not overlook the disapproval of her mother, who conveyed the message that good little girls are not supposed to display such exuberance as she did when she jumped up and hugged her father.

Claiming to be too afraid of the dark to sleep alone, she would go to her parents' bed, where her father welcomed her but his wife complained about being made uncomfortable. She then went to her brother's bedroom and crept into his bed without waking him. When he found her there, he teased her about being a "scaredy cat," and his taunt, so at odds with her exaggerated sense of entitlement, shamed and infuriated her. She then tried sleeping on the floor at the foot of her parents' bed and was shamed by the objections this raised.

When she was six or seven, she got involved with "doctor games," which she enjoyed but which made her feel guilty. When she confessed this activity to her mother, she was sternly reprimanded and warned that if she did this again her mother would tell her father. As a result of being shamed in this way, she channeled all her vivacity and exuberance into athletic activities. Although she excelled in these, she failed to achieve as an athlete because she withdrew from competition, partly for fear of being envied and partly because she felt that success would gratify her mother too much.

As she entered puberty she resented the development of her breasts and was embarrassed by her menses. Her appearance and personality made her very popular with boys during adolescence, but she dated only because it was expected of her. She disliked kissing and quickly ended her relationship with any boy who exhibited a real interest in her. When her girlfriends spoke of their experiences with boys, she reacted inwardly with wonder at their behaving in a way that would be repugnant to her.

As time went on, she stopped dating, denied having any sexual feelings, and felt awkward in any social situation involving the opposite sex. She avoided all physical contact and drew away from her father when he tried to be affectionate. I hope that without giving any further details I have demonstrated that this patient's problems had gone beyond the original oedipal conflict and now included a feeling of not being entitled to be a woman or to have sexual feelings, and that this nonentitlement was based on feelings of shame induced by her mother's excessive disapproval. A therapeutic clarification of her oedipal conflict would not be enough to bring about a change in her behavior; her attitude of nonentitlement was ego-syntonic at this point, and required working through before her sexual and feminine feelings could be expected to emerge. Hers is a case in which exaggerated entitlement attitudes, psychological and social, leading to an expectation of acceptance and approval, coexisted with attitudes of nonentitlement in an area essential to the sense of identity.

My second example is the case of a highly successful professional man in his fifties who came to see me because of periods of intense anxiety and depression. He had been seen in the past by two other psychiatrists and had been hospitalized for depression. Although he maintained that he would be better off dead, there was no evidence of suicidal intent, nor had he made suicidal gestures. His anxiety seemed to dominate over his depression, which I assessed as being secondary to his sense of hopelessness. This intuition was confirmed by our psychological procedure, the Psychodynamic and Therapeutic Evaluation (PaTE Report), which indicated the presence of severe anxiety but demonstrated no evidence of suicidal feelings.

His father was a master mechanic, an ardent union supporter who had always felt inferior in a world he perceived as being highly stratified along class lines. He felt that the rich had everything, and that all the trouble in the world arose from their keeping everything for themselves. As a boy my patient had observed his father's deferential, obsequious, and self-abasing manner in the presence of those he considered important and prominent. His father, whose schooling had stopped with the fourth grade, felt inferior to his wife, who had completed high school, so he left their child's rearing to her. When the patient or his brothers had appealed to their father, protesting their mother's strict, domineering, and judgmental attitude in some particular, he would reply,

"Be a man, son. Do as your mother tells you." The mother was morose and openly belittling of her husband. There were many quarrels about their way of life and about money. A third son, my patient sensed very early in life that his mother had wanted a girl; she gave him a nickname that was in effect a masculine version of the name he would have been given had he been a girl. He was the good boy, however, his mother's helper, and he identified with her. A good student, he nevertheless doubted his intelligence and ability. His development had progressed appropriately enough on the surface, with success in school, the acquisition of friends, and participation in various sports; but he always hesitated to ask the most popular girls for dates. He did well in college, where he met a girl who took an interest in him and whom he married. The couple had children, and he became successful professionally. Why, then, did he have the anxiety and depression he manifested in the initial stages of his analysis, primarily in his reaction to me? He was profoundly concerned about being accepted and approved of and expressed considerable trepidation about saying or revealing anything that would antagonize or alienate me. In one way or another he tried to assess what would please me. It was evident that he sought to be the perfect patient so that I would take a particular interest in him. He feared that I would proclaim that there was something so seriously wrong with him that he would be untreatable.

The feeling of there being "something wrong" with him was one of a lack, of something missing, of an emptiness or void associated with a vague sense of shame he could not define. Further investigation revealed that my patient was seeking some confirmation or validation, chiefly from a woman. This quest was accompanied by fairly intense anxiety, of which he was aware, and by severe rage, which was primarily denied or repressed and little acknowledged. He did question his manliness, although in actuality he had no difficulty performing the sex act. The problem was that he doubted being a man enough to satisfy a woman.

The reason for his feeling of having "something wrong" with himself became apparent in a very interesting way. One day this quite dignified, distinguished man told me that while driving to his session with me he had been struck with the thought that he would "like to rape all those god-damned women." He wondered aloud if he had not wanted to rape his mother. When I asked what that would have meant to him, he replied that it would have shown her who was boss. I wondered if his being boss meant that she would then have accepted him as a man. He wholeheartedly agreed, and then said, "My father had a right to die; my mother didn't have the right to die." This brought out the fact that his father had accepted him as a man, but that his mother had never really put her stamp of approval on him but had cheated him out of his birthright. At the same time, he recognized that he had enjoyed being mother's pet, and while growing up he had not liked certain manly activities. He then spoke of how he had identified with his mother, and this led to the recognition of his great efforts to be "mother's girl" while at the same time resenting her failure to recognize him as a boy and then a man. He claimed that the constant quarrels between his parents would not have taken place if he had "come out right" and been born a girl; so what was wrong with him was that he had "come out wrong" and been a boy when he should have been a girl. This was further confirmed by a repeating fantasy he had before falling asleep, in which an utterly beautiful woman found him extremely attractive and affectionately attached herself to him and totally took care of him, relieving him of all responsibility and enabling him to do anything he wanted. This fantasy involved no actual sexual behavior; it was a rebirth fantasy in which he was unconditionally accepted and nurtured and needed no longer to be concerned about his lovability, acceptability, or worth—one in which he finally "came out right."

From the moment of his birth this man clearly sensed that something was lacking in his relationship to the significant other, his mother. Although he was cared for and nurtured, the appropriate degree of tenderness was lacking. Normal processes of development, of individuation and separation, took place, but along with this, his sense of lack persisted and grew into the notion that something was wrong. In the infant's and child's self-referential system, this translated into "something's wrong with me." The feeling that he had "come out wrong" became the basis of his conviction that he would be tolerated only if he gratified the significant other, his mother. As the patient put it himself, "I always felt I owed my mother something," so from early life he felt that his worth was contingent on how he behaved. If he was not too much trouble, if he did what he was told to do, if he was helpful, then he might be loved and the tenderness he missed would be forthcoming. By being the good boy he partially gratified his need for tenderness, avoided punishment and rejection, and did develop a tentative self. With his excellent native endowment he was able to mature intellectually and physically, but he remained on a contingent basis emotionally and never developed a sense of being a person in his own right. To put it in other words, he was never entitled to feel that he had any basic rights as a person but always had to prove himself and justify his existence. This indebtedness to his mother became an indebtedness to the world. This attitude of nonentitlement not only was based on psychological grounds but had been culturally inculcated also by his working-class background, in which he had heard it declared that "the rich have everything; we working people have to suffer." This insight was confirmed by the patient's recalling that he had gone into acute anxiety at the purchase of his first car and, later, when he bought his first house. He had asked himself, "Who am I to own this?" The major therapeutic task is always to help such patients to grasp with insight and emotion that such attitudes are not ego-syntonic but actually ego-alien; that they undermine self-esteem and enslave them, never freeing them to become the persons they are capable of being and to really enjoy living. This may be partly accomplished by appropriate interpretations, but essentially it is a question of the transference relationship to the therapist that results in a corrective emotional experience.

The major problem in the transference is not who is the central transference figure, which usually in these cases is the mother. The analyst is placed in the idealized mother role, and the patient constantly seeks to be the perfect patient and is terrified that if he makes a mistake the analyst will totally reject him and discover his innate badness. The maternal transference aspects in the course of treatment are not too difficult to resolve. The problem comes afterwards in that the nonentitlement feelings are so ego-syntonic that the patient can never see himself as an equal human being. For example, I replaced three pictures on one of the walls in my office. The patient could not miss seeing these pictures, yet he never expressed any curiosity about them until I raised the question as to why he never said anything. He explained he did not feel he had any right to know anything personal about the analyst. When the analyst inquired further, the patient recalled the frequent childhood experiences of being excluded from serious family discussions and decisions. Because of the ego-syntonic nature of his feelings of nonentitlement, these feelings recurred innumerable times in the transference, for example, in the patient's reluctance to request appointment changes and his timidity when meeting the analyst outside the office. Each time these situations occurred they were reworked with further genetic material unfolding. Finally, he was able to resolve this aspect of his character neurosis and express his views, opinions, and questions in a direct manner.

I hope that I have demonstrated my thesis in these two illustrations and have made it clear that attitudes of entitlement are bimodal in origin. All human beings have entitlement attitudes that can be classified into three groups: attitudes of normal and exaggerated entitlement and the attitude of nonentitlement. If the latter two do not involve the sense of identity, they are but minor, and should be considered simply egocentricities. If, however, they do involve the sense of identity, they are major factors in the psychopathology of the person in question and are bimodal (social and psychological) in origin. Therapeutically, nonentitlement attitudes are more insidious and difficult to uncover and pinpoint than are attitudes of exaggerated entitlement. These latter attitudes are more readily recognized in the therapeutic situation because they involve essentially acts of commission. The patient proclaims or behaves in a manner which clearly demonstrates his exaggerated attitudes of what he has a right to, even though he may be unaware that his behavior is reality dystonic.

In contrast, attitudes of nonentitlement primarily involve acts of omission; where action should have been taken, there is none, and since this is ego-syntonic, the patient is unaware of his rights and the therapist may also not realize that there is an omission. As one patient stated, "I feel I am entitled to a certain recognition. I do not feel entitled to ask or request this recognition, but if I don't get it I feel righteously indignant." The therapist may only hear the exaggerated entitlement attitude of righteous indignation which is verbalized, and not realize the underlying nonverbalized attitude of nonentitlement. This can be particularly true in geriatric cases involving a person who at one time had reached a level of some renown in his particular occupation. Now, in his retirement, he is no longer productive and thus experiences a loss of his sense of identity, accompanied by the feeling he is no longer entitled. The therapist, however, perceives the patient in terms of his past achievement, expects him to feel normally entitled, and thus overlooks the nonentitlement attitudes in spite of being aware that the patient has experienced some loss of identity.

It is due to the negative nature of nonentitlement attitudes that they have not been clinically recognized or investigated as much as attitudes of exaggerated entitlement. Recognition of these factors should help the therapist to understand why some individuals from deprived backgrounds seem able to rise above the environmental deficits and why others with apparently the whole world in the palms of their hands flounder and never develop into what they could have been. Entitlement attitudes can be a major motivating force in the person's development of his inner resources and his sense of identity or a marked hindrance to his sense of worth and acceptance of himself as a person in his own right. Although social factors are important influences in the development of entitlement attitudes, my clinical experience has shown that early developmental experiences, particularly the relationship to the mother and the degree to which she appropriately mirrors her child, are pivotal.

REFERENCES

Diagnostic and statistical manual of mental disorders (DSM III). 1980. 3d ed. Washington, D.C.: The American Psychiatric Association.

Freud, S. 1916. Some character types met within psychoanalytic work. In *Standard edition*, 14:309–33. London: Hogarth Press, 1964.

Horney, K. 1950. *Neurosis and human growth*. New York: W. W. Norton.

Jacobson, E. 1959. The "exceptions": An elaboration of Freud's character study. In *The psychoanalytic study of the child,* 14:135–54. New York: International Universities Press.

Kriegman, G., and L. Kriegman. 1965. The PaTE report: A new psychodynamic and therapeutic evalaution procedure, Parts I and II. *Psychiat. Q.* 39:646–74.

———. 1970. *The PaTE report manual*. 2d rev. ed. Richmond: G. Kriegman and L. Kriegman.

Levin, S. 1967. Some metapsychological considerations on the differentiation between shame and guilt. *Int. J. Psycho-Anal.* 48:267–76.

Levin, S. 1970. On psychoanalysis of attitudes of entitlement. *Bull. Phila. Assn. Psychoanal.* 20:1–10.

Murray, J. 1964. Narcissism and the ego ideal. *J. Am. Psychoanal. Assn.* 12:477–511.

Pierce, C. M. 1978. Entitlement dysfunctions. *Aust. N.Z. J. Psychiat.* 12:215–19.

Rothstein, A. 1977. The ego attitude of entitlement. *Int Rev. Psycho-Anal.* 4:409–17.

Solomon, I., and S. Leven. 1975. Entitlement. *Psychother. Theory, Res. Pract.* 12:280–85.

2.

Entitlement: Some Developmental Perspectives

Robert M. Dorn

Entitlement and Development

I n the three to four years of life leading up to oedipal issues, infant toddlers, and parenting caretakers, have to work out critical social issues of boundaries between what is inside oneself (me/my) and what is outside. Debates begin between one's own rights and the rights of others. Needs and wants inevitably conflict with other peoples' interpretations of rights, needs, and wants. Attachment-detachment themes are recurrent. A social setting that provides opportunities for observation of this social transactional field richly demonstrates how value systems are shaped and modified on the spectrum from self-serving, egoistic behavior to social behavior concerning others, with all its rewards and punishments. An infant's drives and value system are shaped early on. They are continually modified through social and cultural exchanges, first with mother, father, and surrogates and, in the second and third years, through social and cultural exchanges with other caretakers and other toddlers. Siblings have a lot to say to each other and more often than not say it in action as well as words. Levin (1970) speaks of attitudes of restricted entitlement and describes how parental intrusions into the child's growing sphere of ego activities can severely restrict, curb, and shape what the person feels entitled to do, have, and be.

Levin provides a case example of how parents' rights created a lifelong character style of restricted entitlement. His patient, a thirty-five-year-old businessman, characteristically lived a role of deferring to others, for example, toward a business partner and in his analytic transference relationship. In his analysis, the family antecedents showed that father, a prominent political person, expected his children to glorify his position and promote his ambition. Mother saw herself as the power behind the throne. The children were stunted. Levin states that none "has a mature sense of freedom to find his own way in life or to develop his own interest" (8–9).

Kriegman (1983), also addressing restricted entitlement and nonentitlement, points to the work of Margaret Mahler and her colleagues (1975) and suggests that disturbances in the symbiotic phase create the psychological matrix for those adult character traits. He suggests they occur due to maternal deficiencies and failures to provide an adequate ambience and nurturance to convey a sense of worth.

It might be more accurate to refer to these problems as difficulties of differentiation from the symbiotic phase (specifically separation-individuation subphases). The separation-individuation model is clinically useful but seems to lack transactional clinical applicability for some psychoanalysts without child training. On the other hand, object relations language lends itself to clinical explorations of transference and countertransference issues within the transference analysis. Using an object relations model, my developmental hypotheses will now be described as they have emerged within the clinical frames of two analyses. Transferences (and countertransferences) provide action models between the patient and the analyst and point out transactional models with others. In the instances to be described, action models between therapist and patient are here-and-now existential experiences, essential to checking out what has been disturbed, or destroyed, and essential to initiating change. They are testable in the clinical situation and relatively uncomplicated.

Winnicott's (1965) "good-enough mother" (145, 146) and "adequate holding environment" (47) provide a cushion for slowly dawning disillusionment throughout the infant-toddler years. Socialization processes tear away illusions of perpetual self-rights and proprietary ownership. The democratic concepts so neatly laid out in *Robert's Rules of Order* have their origins in the action discourses of family life and during the nursery school era of development. The actual practice of these concepts is fragile and easily overrun by the egoistic, self-serving attitudes of either infant-toddler or parent/parent surrogate.

Winnicott's work on transitional phenomena (1953), his later work with Stevenson (1954), and his paper on the location of cultural experience (1966) express socialization phenomena in microscopic, developmental, and psychoanalytic terms. Drinking/feeding orality from birth, as an actual biologic-physiologic process of rooting-sucking, on and in the presence of mother (with all her smells, sights, touch sensations, and sounds), is soon enlarged to include fingers, and/or thumb, and snout area and becomes a complex sensorimotor, kinaesthetic, and psychologic process. Somewhere between four to twelve months postpartum, attachments may occur to some special object (a cloth or a blanket), further enlarging the repertoire of experiences.

These parenting adults and infants have made a basic psychological discovery. The body and mind have the capacity to manufacture or create antianxiety states using either or both fingers-thumbs and external materials. Parents can supply the objects when it seems advisable. Infants have the option of demanding their rights and their entitlements. Textures and smells can be recreated; new object-substitutes can be developed by parents. Infants may or may not accept replacements. A new series of dialogues and actions result in further discoveries and creations. While they usually fail to substitute for the actual parent, they do work. Because maturation is slow, the usefulness of this shared creativity can hardly be overstated. During this period these object-substitutes assist in the struggle to gain independence and in a balanced feeling between one's own needs and the slowly dawning realization of desires and rights as defined by others.

As stated earlier, this interim period leading to an awareness of this social interpersonal interpretation of reality is potentially fraught with grievous disillusionments. The infant-toddler learns that he is not the center of the universe. The world with all its wonderments does not exist solely to provide and care for him or her.

However, reviewed from another perspective, it is a period of marked potential for psychological and social growth. Psychologically and socially, a capacity for creativity has been discovered. A repertoire of material derivatives is gradually manufactured. The "pacifier" and transitional blanket-objects such as teddy bears and toys, in conjunction with body-part activities, are the building blocks for external daydream-playactions and internal fantasy-daydream developments. These are both interpersonal-transactional (group play) and solitary (hand, mouth, and body surface parts and orifices autoerotisms with sensations, affects, and fantasies).

Socially, there is a true beginning of give and take. Reciprocity can be practiced. Entitlement issues and affects stirred up by disagreements create opportunities for "conversations." Quarrels or disagreements, negotiations, refusals to work at the shared bargaining tables, usually followed by making-up and patching-over, are practicing derivatives described by many infant psychologists and infant-toddler psychoanalysts and are well-known to parents.

Psychologically, a social mind and an egoistic mind coexist. Intrapsychic life will be permanently enriched, albeit permanently prone to normal intrapsychic conflict and normal neurotic behavior.

Let's look at the ideal state first. Given the enriched environment provided by nurturing parents, independence-dependence or autonomy is not a question that needs to be faced yet. Transitional spaces can be explored and enjoyed without any question as to who created them. "They're just there." Winnicott (1966) calls the "things" in this space "me-extensions" and the "subjective object," in contrast to the adult's perception of the person interacting with the baby as the "object objectively perceived" (371). What is critical for my thesis is the permission the caregiver provides and the nature of the creativity provided by such entitlement experiences. People continue to use new soothers into adulthood, and creative adults continue to play with ideas and things.

Some people will not have been so fortunate. They are the ones who have lost out on entitlement experiences. For reasons as varied as genetic defects, inadequate stimulation, inappropriate stimulation, or gross failures to have boundaries respected, illusions of entitlement are prevented from growing firm and reliable.

There are two types of failures to respect boundaries. One is failure to provide the parenting part of the partnership. It is characterized by severe curtailments of provisions, separations, and loss of opportunities for essential cultural enrichment (the deficiency disorders). The second type is characterized by premature and repetitive intrusions by others into this critical space for reasons other than the infant needs. Physical and sexual abuse represent failures of adults to respect the boundaries and needs of the infant-child. Holding-providing functions are destroyed when spatial boundaries are not respected. Such exploitations destroy a sense of entitlement, even if it is already relatively well developed. Consider adult victims of abuse. Each person can attest to the degree of long-term, even chronic, damage to entitlement and self-esteem that occurs after personal space boundaries are traumatically violated. Incest and rape victims, adult as well as child, often suffer *alone* for years, unable to feel, let alone express, righteous indignation and rage. When such appropriate affects do begin to appear, we start to talk of "improvement" and think of this as signaling the return of entitlement sensibilities. Self-worth and self-esteem may be permanently fragile, even after adult rape of the adult. What must be the sensations, experiences, and consequences within the infant-child victim?

A Psychoneurotic Character Deformation

A patient, married and mother of three, came for psychoanalysis, claiming an inability to follow through and complete things (inhibitions) and lack of certainty as to what it was she wanted to be and accomplish (identity problems). She had started an analysis shortly after graduating from college. As she would reconstruct it, based on insights she and I were able to put together during the first two years of analysis: "Somehow I was able to convince my father that my analyst and the process were bad for me." Her father became her "agent" and stopped it for her.

After two years of analysis with me, when she had reached the age of thirty-four, her identity boundaries were clarified enough for us to see the degree to which ego-functions were impaired by her need to disavow goals for herself. Having children had helped modify goal achievement. She could fight on her children's behalf and feel they were entitled to accomplishments and gratifications. However, when similar entitlement issues on her own behalf came into focus, displacements, inhibitions, and disavowals occurred.

Feelings of possessiveness were denied but began to occur in the transference. For example, she felt the psychiatry residents where I was working got more of me, not that she wanted more. In fact, she had thoughts and feelings that some of the things coming up in her analysis (her products) were useful in my teaching and were helping the residents be better psychiatrists. I was taking her productions and giving them to others. However, twinges of affect occurred as she provided things for us. Could she object (not that she did)? Did she have that privilege (entitlement)? Once again, disavowal occurred: "Whether I do or not, it really doesn't matter."

She began to compare herself with her younger brother, Paul. She is not comfortable spending money; he is. She will fly on the night flight to save money. He will go first class. As she feels envy and rage, she sees a perfect character for herself represented in a movie: "She's ugly, fat, with a dirty face, hiding in the background. She is so upset, just like I am upset with Paul, who seems able to pull it off and get away with it." She sees him with a smug face, while she feels deprived and envious. This time, she can't blame it on others: she is doing it to herself. It is she who's "making a mess of things."

In childhood, Paul adored her and followed her around like a shadow. She enjoyed having him so clearly at her beck and call. As he grew older, and taller, and began to develop interest beyond the two of them, it was as if parts of herself were going away. Memories appeared of all his specialness, not only to her but to her father as well. She made statements such as: "I get this feeling that Paul has special entitlements, and it pisses me off. I think if I could get some control over him, if I could develop a domination over him, I could share in his power. Even as a kid it felt that way. He outgrew me, and he's no longer under my control. I still feel envy when his wife will say something and he responds to her instead of me."

In order to avoid dealing forthrightly with issues of entitlement relating to herself, she has, since adulthood, dealt with them in terms of envy and efforts to develop affiliations with "powerful people." Boyfriends, and later her husband, became the repositories.

In her analysis she described how she still continued to take a soother to bed when by herself. If alone she took a pillow to bed and held it while falling asleep. The word *pillow* became useful to describe mental representations of the repository areas for hurt, revengeful feelings and fantasies, and reparation behavior around key issues of loss. Analytic hours were "pillows" of varying degrees of cushioning, which later in the analysis were seen as protecting me and others from fantasies of rage and revenge. As the analysis continued there were ample occasions to see my interpretive powers as changing from "useful," similar to her father who could do no wrong, to relatively "useless."

As reconstructed by me, and later confirmed by her, infant-toddlerhood times were extremely painful, and now the analysis was failing to protect her and me from pain. Entitlement issues became prominent in the transference. Prior to this both patient and love objects had been relatively protected by curtailment of expectations, intrapsychically and interpersonally. But now her two worlds of object representations and of interpersonal relationships became increasing divided into those with power, authority, and entitlement and those without. Powerful affects, sensations, and moods began to emerge with accompanying fantasies and memories as transference issues dealt with long-standing conflicts and defenses. Idealization had given way to the crucial question of whether my capacity to provide adequate "cushions" to her disillusionments would suffice to allow us to examine the consequences of her regressively revived and unrequited feelings of entitlement.

Restricted Entitlement and Nonentitlement

A colleague had a man, Professor X, in psychoanalysis for several years. Both analyst and patient agreed they had reached a stalemate. The analyst felt this was due to an unconscious collusion between Professor and Mrs. X. Without her entering therapy, unconscious transferences between the couple precluded essential materials coming into the husband's analysis. As the wife viewed it, she started an analysis with me to further her husband's analytic work. She felt "he was an impossible person" and kept hoping that further analysis would improve their marriage.

Space only permits an overview of this very challenging analytic patient. Freud's comment on the instincts seeming "to be sleeping" (1964) certainly fit her very well. She and her husband had developed an ideal use of splitting mechanisms. All the bad and all the brilliance were in him. Despite outstanding professional talents he was persona non grata socially and in professional circles. She was pitied by people who knew them. His temper, abuse, and need to dominate were well-known. Yet, to call this a sadomasochistic relationship does not adequately describe the complex nature of her relationship to him and others.

The analysis was tedious. Many times, I wonder what motivated her and me to continue. She reminded me of McDougall's antianalysands (1980). Her college goals had been only partially fulfilled. In career development and socially, she was inhibited. She hated the semirural urban area where they had settled and longed to return to a seacoast region where each of them had grown up. During the analysis, they bought a small weekend place on the Pacific coast, which evoked the first signs of enthusiasm I noticed in her. She certainly did not exhibit any about her home life, her marriage, social relationships, or the analytic work we hoped we were doing.

Each week she had long lists of things to get done, having to do with her three children, ages seven, nine, and eleven, the house, the household pets, and the family automobiles. Lists, and needs of others, clearly lowered priorities having to do with her and, as the analysis proceeded, lowered priorities having to do with us.

I began to feel myself objecting whenever "we" received a demotion in priority, and I began to speak up on behalf of "us." I told her I felt one of us had to be the spokesperson on behalf of her/me and "our rights." Why was it always somebody else or something else who got priority consideration?

However, during the second year, some changes began to occur. I could feel her growing enthusiasm for certain activities and relationships. One was horseback riding, and another was time at the beach house. I felt reassured and heartened. Possibly she and I were finally onto something that heretofore was more or less "dead" inside her. I shared with her my hypothesis that her relationships with the two horses she had purchased and with the beach, the house, and its surroundings were bringing us into contact with parts of herself and significant others, as places, activities, and individuals, in reality or fantasy, formerly unrecognized, but very important. Could it be that these were bits and parts of how she felt about herself and her mother before her next sibling was born (when she was about two years old)? Was it after two that she began to disown her enthusiasms and longings for these special being mothered/mothering experiences? Were we tracking back into the first two years of life, where sensations of excitement and pleasure existed with some mothering person?

She definitely had been providing it all these years, first for her husband, and then for her three children, and certainly for the household pets and the barnyard animals. The horses were recent acquisitions and represented a small part of her latency period passion for collecting miniature toy horses.

In reality, the two horses were mavericks, very unpredictable and hard to handle (more like her husband than herself). During the analysis, they became somewhat more tractable and predictable. It was possible for others to ride them, but they were clearly "her" horses. They responded to her regular attention and to her irregularities or inability to be regular. I drew an analogy between her and them and her and me as represented in her analysis. Their responsiveness to being attended to or neglected represented heretofore absent responses to entitlement issues.

Nonetheless, her horses and her analysis (and I) were still predominately neglected for others. Still I felt hopeful that some progress toward entitlement was taking place. Mrs. X began to seek more pleasure by way of the beach place. She stood up for her children's and her rights to have some summer time there. She would guiltily confess her sense of disloyalty, as she described her excitement at going to the coast. She said: "If I could only take you to the beach with me, and we could be analyzing there; then everything would be complete."

My reply was to point out that at this stage, it probably was much more important to identify those bits and pieces of her enthusiasms and to learn what revived them for her, rather than to insist they had to take place only here with us. At the same time, I told her I was convinced that the analysis was central to this resuscitation process. Without it, I doubted if she would ever have been able to withstand the forces working to make priority lists, with herself constantly being demoted and bumped off.

In time, it became clear that more than guilt was responsible for the massive amnesias and defenses. Transference experiences were very weak. By examining her use of transitional materials, experiences, and displacements to things, to animals, and to others, she and I were able to determine how much hurt, anger, and spitefulness remained within her to be revengefully expressed by keeping me outside, making me wait, and dragging out the analytic process. I do not believe that it was only I who was outside. It felt as if I also represented important parts of her entitlement issues for herself, and they too were not to be fulfilled. Mrs. X and I may have to settle for far less of an analytic experience than other people experience. All damage is not necessarily reversible. After only two plus years of analysis I cannot speak from hindsight. Only a return to experiencing entitlement issues in the analysis will tell how much can be brought back into a living transference.

A painful incident that happened to her graphically described all of this in the language of dream symbolism and its references to early childhood, body parts, affects, and spaces. She rarely reported dreams, but one day she came to her session very upset and shared with me the fact that her bicycle had been stolen.

This is what transpired: "Good morning, it's not such a good morning. My bike was stolen right out of our walled-in garden. It's a high wall, well over my head. It had to be deliberate. Nothing else was taken. Why didn't they take the tandem bicycle? Maybe it was too hard to move. *I have a violated feeling. It's very upsetting. After I spent so much time selecting just the right one.*"

With questioning from me, the patient went on to describe some of the bicycle's fine details (its gear system, its special custom-made seat, the bike gloves) "All the things I considered made it mine. Just the way I wanted it to be."

She next described further details, as they occurred to her. For example, "how both the front and rear wheels can be taken off so it can be rapidly placed in a small box and taken from place to place in a small car." She went on to say that it "triggered off a strange dream."

The manifest dream was as follows: "I'm checking the back yard. I'm sensing something is gone. Despite locking up things, just like in reality, someone got into the service area, the place where the garbagemen take the trash, which isn't where I left the bike. Could it be one of them? I hate to think so. In the first segment of the dream I go out to check. It looks bare, more so than in reality . . . almost swept clean. The woodpile is left, and a cactus collection. Both the bike that I really lost and the tandem are there. As I look about I notice that the wrought-iron door has missing parts, like someone has blown a big hole in it. As I look again, it looks like chaos. The bike is there, but it's all in pieces. The next-door neighbors have done it. They were doing it, planning to fix things up, but were unaware of what they are doing to things. The wood fence in the backyard has become a brick fence, and is now all in sections. You can see through, and it's all fixed the wrong way." The patient adds an affect of anger at the careless way the bikes have been stacked.

She went on to say that the side of the house where this breaking up of things had been going on is the side of the house where the neighbor family lives with whom they have had problems. The man of that house and the patient's husband have not got on well at all. She returned to the dream, commenting on a later segment. "Like a flash, I don't know where I was, Michael [her husband] is with me. Suddenly you appear. I can't remember your name. You don't look like you. If anything you look like Dr. Smith [her husband's analyst]. Then I remember your name. You are very short, about 4 foot 2 inches. You have white hair, a gold tweed sport jacket, a Shetland sweater, plaid pants. The white hair is really shockingly white, like Andy Warhol's used to look. I'm not sure but I think there was a bridge over a brook nearby."

The patient went on to comment that in the dream there is no sense of reaction, like people having rights, or a sense of indignation, a sense of entitlement, or a sense of recourse. She described herself as being more of an observer, like looking at something with maybe some irritation (playing down the affect). I asked her if there was a sense of indifference?

She replied: "That isn't it. It's a sense of being not involved. I just wasn't involved in doing something about it." As she talked, she starts musing about the local city police department. "I have some doubt about their honesty. . . . I think they could even be a part of the action."

Further conversation between us about involvement/uninvolvement, caring/indifference, led to the idea of someone being a reporter, taking notes of the incident, and mentioning it to her husband, or someone like him, "He'd be the active one. When I mentioned something about this incident to him, he exploded."

This gave me an opportunity to talk about partnership. Her husband is the active, expressive one. It is the ying/yang of the circle. Together they make the whole, complementing each other. To what degree was her attraction to him due to his ability to be the expressor and a way around her own block against expressing indignation? Was there capacity for righteous indignation under these circumstances?

Now she began to express affect. "I didn't feel I had done wrong. It's our yard. People who do things like that should be strung up. . . . I struggle with the difference between me and those people who can intrude into private spaces where they're not invited." She talks about "violators, takers. . . . A population I didn't know about, growing up."

Association led to Jewishness and anti-Semitism. Once again she was able to disengage herself by saying that "growing up I didn't have the kind of experiences my daughters have had here." Yesterday her younger daughter heard a derogatory remark from some girl about being Jewish. "This was Alicia's [the younger daughter's] first experience with the Jewish problem. *I used to excuse people. I used to make excuses for them.* What comes to mind is a person across the street who hurt Cary [her older daughter]. Her mother wouldn't let her daughter play with her. First she made all kinds of excuses, little bits and pieces or reasons why she couldn't play with her. Gradually the bits and pieces fit together so that it was obvious that it was because she was Jewish. *Cary was crushed.*"

As I listened to the patient describing this, it sounded increasingly like words had not yet developed in our vocabulary to describe the area we were entering. The stealing of the bicycle had precipitated things. The robbery had catapulted us into areas still outside and best represented in current affects on behalf of her daughters.

Intruders, violators, individuals taking the prerogative to exclude ingenuous children from participating in play activities because they are Jewish were stirring up righteous indignation on behalf of others. She sees one of her daughters, Cary, "crushed," by the denigration. The younger daughter, Alicia, can overcome hurts and injuries. The other becomes devastated by them.

I asked her which one she is more like. She said that superficially she may appear to be more like the one who can take it. I said it appeared to me that inside herself she was devastated and, before we began to work on the problem of entitlement, would have come to the conclusion, "Well, there's nothing you can do about it, so why not be philosophical, accept things, and forget about it." Had she some time in the past, possibly early in childhood, come to this conclusion? Had she subsequently more or less backed off, retreated, and avoided further confrontation for herself around these issues?" I told her that it seemed to me that before we had begun our sessions, these areas of righteous indignation, urges to fight back, not let people get away with things, had become more or less dead issues inside of her and overdeveloped in her husband.

She had no words to precisely describe her state of mind. It had something to do with feelings of helplessness or hopelessness, but these were only speculations. Her sister came to mind. She had called yesterday. "Just now I was feeling a motherly feeling toward her and her husband. They may have to move. There is no work for John [her husband] in Seattle. They are leaving, and going to Arizona. Bernice's concern is for our grandparents. She doesn't want to hurt them." All of the children are very caring and concerned for these grandparents. They remain the loved ones, with relatively little manifest ambivalence toward them, in contrast to the aversion felt by the patient toward her mother and the ambivalence felt toward her father.

Once again, I was reminded of McDougall's (1980) work on

the antianalysand. The person has to disown affects due to alienation from his or her own instinctual impulses directed against objects. Fenichel (1945) considered partial behaviors of this type as neurotic. The alienation from the instinctual impulses, the wish to disown them, results in either not feeling them at all, feeling only a part of them, or experiencing them in a distorted way (477).

In my own mind, I wondered to what a degree the patient could be awakened? Was it possible for her and me to penetrate, to get through the wall, into the backyard garden where so much damage was done? Was it possible to revive a sense of entitlement and rights? Language for such feelings had been destroyed or may never have existed. Analysis had provided some language links to feelings of possessiveness and to her actions of acquiring possessions. The robbery had uncovered the fact that these links were already far advanced. Her ambivalent admiration and attraction to her husband were understandable as probably referring to split-off parts of herself.

Was the analytic process going to prove capable of linking up these stimuli in the analytic sessions? The symbolism provided us with evidence suggesting we were penetrating into anal areas, property rights, and affects, heretofore primarily projected out into children and husband. Like the previous patient she could fight like a tigress on behalf of her children's rights and could be all too tolerant of entitlement in her husband. In fact, many people wondered why she stayed married to him. Now evidence was accumulating to make this comprehensible.

She and I began to pay more attention to her possessions. The detailed care and interest in the custom-made bicycle afforded us one more possession to land on an accumulating beachhead of transitional objects of adulthood. These were adding up to a growing sense of rights and entitlements and affects of indignation when people violated her territory and her spaces.

Was I becoming the potentially nurturing parent transference object? Were we exploring transitional spaces (re-)externalized, and were the bicycle, beach house, horses, barnyard animals, household pets, and even daughters, and now I, similar to Winnicott's (1966) "me-extensions" and "subjective-objects?" However we name them, they, she/I, and we/us were stimulating powerful affects. Dead issues were clearly not totally dead, and "sleeping dogs" were no longer totally dormant.

Previous experiences with similar patients have forced me to lose much of my early enthusiastic belief that such people could always be helped. There have been too many occasions when the transference transactions have proved to me that bitterness subsequent to early hurts, mistrust, hate, and revenge preclude a good outcome. Sometimes the need to live out affects of despair and hopelessness and fantasies of revenge are too great. Sometimes unconscious fantasies that come alive in the transference prove emancipating from their former use in projective identifications. But frequently old interpersonal relations prove too strong, and pathological compromises remain anchored within the context of former adaptations.

Like immigrants to America, it's as if much of their hope and optimism have become almost totally invested in the next generation. Their children should have it better than they did, while they themselves, given the second chance of analysis, decide to settle for far less than their talents promise and the analyst deems possible. There are occasions when sleeping dogs seem stirred, only to go back to sleep.

Prevention

The results of severely damaging early-in-life experiences may not be fully reversible. However, psychic epigenesis is not as rigidly fixed as previously thought, and character development is increasingly seen as a lifelong process. This raises the question of the value of early intervention in preventing lasting and irreversible psychic damage, including damage regarding entitlement issues.

There is currently an ongoing research project designed to study mentally ill mothers and their children under five years of age (the Chicago-based Threshold Mothers Project). Its goal is to study factors surrounding vulnerability, resiliency, and response to intervention efforts. This work by Musick et al. (1987) has deminstrated a constellation of maternal factors that appear to be related to the child's capacity to seek and use growth-promoting influences beyond the mother's orbit. These children were able to turn to significant others within the therapeutic nursery environment and to use positively what was offered to enhance their further development. In an oversimplified fashion, one might say these mothers, although disabled, have provided positive, encouraging, and growth-fostering factors. During crises these mothers appear to be less selfish and to allow their children to move beyond their orbit. Such a mother, rather than narcissistically tying her child to herself for her own needs and nurturance, helped her child to feel entitled to more because she felt he was entitled to more. The authors designated this capacity as "enablement."

These mothers were sensitively aware that some of their children's problems were due to degrees of understimulation, repeated separations, and exposure to an environment not always predictable. Despite feeling hurt that others could give what they were not able to provide, they followed through, were consistent, and saw that their children had the benefits of an additional environment to their own. Although possibly consciously aware of a teacher's increasingly exalted position over their own, they proved able to work with teachers on behalf of their child and simultaneously continued to improve their own parenting skills.

39

REFERENCES

Bowlby, J. 1969. *Attachment and loss*. Vol. 1: *Attachment*. New York: Basic Books.

———. 1973. *Attachment and loss*. Vol. 2: *Separation*. New York: Basic Books.

Fenichel, O. 1945. *The psychoanalytic theory of neurosis*. New York: Norton.

Freud, S. 1964. Analysis terminable and interminable. In *Standard edition*, 23:209–53. London: Hogarth Press.

Kriegman, G. 1983. Entitlement attitudes: psychosocial and therapeutic implications. *J. Am. Acad. Psychoanal.* 11:265–81.

Kris, E. 1955. Neutralization and sublimation. In *The psychoanalytic study of the child*, 10:30–46. New York: International Universities Press.

Levin, S. 1970. On psychoanalysis of attitudes of entitlement. *Bull. Phila. Assn. Psychoanal.* 20:1–10.

McDougall, J. 1980. The antianalysand in analysis. In *Plea for a measure of abnormality*, 213–46. New York: International Universities Press.

Mahler, M., F. Pine, and A. Bergman. 1975. *The psychological birth of the human infant*. New York: Basic Books.

Musick, J. S., et al. 1987. The capacity for "enabling" in mentally ill mothers. In *The Invulnerable child*, ed. E. J. Anthony and B. Cohler, 227–52. New York: Guilford.

Stevenson, O., and D. W. Winnicott. 1954. The first treasured possession: A study of the part played by specially loved objects and toys in the lives of certain children. In *The psychoanalytic study of the child*, 9:209–17. New York: International Universities Press.

Winnicott, D. W. 1953. Transitional objects and transitional phenomena: A study of the first not-me possession. *Int. J. Psycho-Anal.* 34:89–97.

———. 1965. *The maturational processes and the facilitating environment*: New York: International Universities Press.

———. 1967. The location of cultural experience. *Int. J. Psycho-Anal.* 48:368–72.

3.

The Psychology of Hope
and the Modification
of Entitlement
near the End of Life

Michel Silberfeld

THE END OF LIFE brings a pointed if not critical perspective of the examination of entitlement attitudes. In the Western biblical tradition reminders of our mortality have been evoked as an antidote to vanity and hubris.

> What profit hath a man of all of his labour which he taketh under the sun?
> One generation passeth away and another generation cometh: but the earth abideth forever.

For in much wisdom is much grief: and he that increaseth
knowledge increaseth sorrow. [Ecclesiastes 1:3, 4, 18]

Even in the confessions of faith, those guided and inspired
answers, the psychological struggles, the pulling apart to divest
oneself of the problems of entitlement are the subject of perennial
scrutiny. In the great literature of the Western world, *The Confessions of Saint Augustine* give a masterful account of the burdens
of the human condition. This is the burden to get beyond oneself,
beyond one's bodily interment, beyond mere worldly preoccupa-
tions. "I may win the mastery, as He has won the mastery over
me, in order that I may be rid of my old temptations and devote
myself only to God's single purpose, forgetting what I have left
behind. I look forward, not to what lies ahead of me in this life
and will surely pass away, but to my eternal goal" (9.29).

If psychoanalysis has not directly addressed ultimate or tran-
scendent values, it has had much to say about the personal struggle
for human and humane values. Freud (1915) believed that man's
basic narcissism remains even in the face of death. At heart a man
does not feel sorry that he will die; he only feels sorry for the man
next to him. Imbedded in this denial of mortality lies the search-
light for self-worth and self-esteem. The very presence of the unconscious within which time does not exist protects this search-
light. But the recognition of mortality cannot be denied entirely.

Ernest Becker (1973) is correct in documenting the evidence
to support the important role that the recognition of mortality
plays in prompting man's search for meaning. Meanings can be
partially reduced to analytically unearthed hidden meanings, but
the synthetic functions which underwrite that quest for meaning have their own autonomy. In addition, the nature of this synthesis requires defining the existential conditions of man's indi-
viduality within the recognition of finitude. This recognition is
fundamental to man's thrust to bring himself beyond bodily fulfillment. The vicissitudes of instinctual development find their

crowning human achievement in the creation of meaning and the investiture of value projected onto the world. To be sure, the accompanying search to find a symbolic identity becomes a cornerstone of self-worth and self-esteem. This symbolic identity is best revealed in the commitment to values, and this commitment in turn is highlighted by the sense of entitlement.

This speaks for a psychoanalysis of positive attributes beyond defensive, developmental, and adaptive considerations. The attribution of meaning and the formation of values have their own ontological necessity. From the perspective near the end of life, it appears there is more to living than just being alive. Instinctual grasping to apprehend the world does find displaced satisfactions in some of the contents of the synthetic capacity. But synthesis provides more than sublimatory satisfactions. Synthesis allows the external world and the individual's place in it to take shape. Philosophers and mystics may dismiss it all as illusion, which in some sense it undoubtedly is. But it remains to be dismissed. The formation of meaning and the ascription of values may be a developmental task of the years beyond the development of abstract reasoning. Inasmuch as other developmental processes gradually achieve some autonomy, so too the creation of meaning may become an end in itself. Near the end of life it is almost a universal, conscious preoccupation. Otherwise it evolves with age. When the prospect of the end of life comes early, it shows similar pseudomature responses as are seen with other developmental tasks undertaken too soon.

But what constitutes entitlement? To answer this question I will take up George Kriegman's (1983) efforts to locate the place of entitlement. Then I will present my thesis to place entitlement within a dynamic psychology of hope.

George Kriegman modified and integrated the subject of entitlement attitudes. As in the beginning of any conceptual program, Kriegman proposed his classification of entitlement attitudes: "normal" entitlement; exaggerated entitlement; and nonentitlement. To quote Kriegman: "As I view entitlement, all persons have equal degrees of entitlement. Some people have unrealistically 'exaggerated' their entitlement and have exaggerated expectations of how others should respond to their wishes. In ... individuals ... [referred to] as having 'restricted attitudes,' I feel a more appropriate term is non-entitlement attitudes because it is not a question so much of restriction, which also has quantitative implications, but of the person questioning his right to any entitlement whatever" (272).

What is the place of entitlement? Kriegman is clear: "Attitudes of exaggerated entitlement or non-entitlement can ... be a major factor in the individual's orientation toward life, a determinant of his sense of identity, and thus of his sense of worth, and result in psychopathology. . . . the etiology of attitudes of entitlement is bimodal: social and psychological" (273).

In this chapter I would like to suggest that the place of entitlement is grounded within a general dynamic psychology of hope. Within this psychology of hope, entitlement plays a special place. Let us elaborate this notion with some clinical material that will animate my speculations.

A Clinical Vignette

The following vignette describes a consultation surrounding a young man dying of a complex medical condition. The consultation points out the necessity to consider questions of entitlement in conjunction with questions of hope which, together, give psychological weight to the nature of loss. Hope, loss, and entitlement constitute an inseparable dynamic triad.

A young man, only nineteen years old, now deceased, had a bone marrow transplantation to treat his refractory leukemia. The transplantation had only half-taken, so that the counts were not good enough for him to leave the hospital yet were high enough to ensure immediate survival. The counts were sufficient for graft versus host disease to be an additional complication.

A call for consultation came, as it turned out, not too long before the young man died. Why then? The tensions around this young man's inability to make full recovery were rising both among and between all of those who were involved. For the family, consisting mainly of a constantly present mother and a frequently visiting father, if their son was not doing well enough, it was because the health-care personnel were not doing more. Perhaps the lack of improvement was even a sign that they were giving up on him. The family was unable in any way to entertain the possibility of their loss. They were opposed in principle to any hint of what they seemed to interpret as defeatism. This made it impossible for them to attend rounds with the medical staff and limited in other ways the possibilities for common interchange. The medical staff had its own difficulties in determining how and where to go with this young man and how to deal with the pressures and limitations of the family. They felt abused by the situation, for they had made considerable efforts not just medically but also personally. Trying as they might to give more, they failed to change the medical outcome or even to win some degree of rewarding appreciation. The family's inability to apprehend the caregivers' plight escalated the tensions for the caregivers. The guilt the family inflicted was persuasive in pushing them beyond what they could really give. The caregivers responded to the exhortations of the parents as to a threat. They all could not accept the inherent helplessness of the situation; the lack of progress must be due to a failure of effort.

As for the young man himself, he made his dilemma quite clear. Every time he thought he was getting better and was about to leave the hospital, there was an additional complication which always prevented his departure. He voiced his desire to live and to keep fighting right up to the very end. Any opportunity to say otherwise was shut off not only by his own conflicted desires but also by the clear unremitting censorship of the family. He must have only a positive attitude! The underside of this attempt to stifle defeatism did sometimes slip out in an expression of fear and discouragement expressed when alone with one of the nurses. In a more veiled manner it was also present in the sometimes not so passive aggressiveness toward the mother. Having seen other similar patients die contributed to a widening discrepancy between the young man's voiced attitude and his evident inaction in caring for himself, which clearly was an emotional statement of a silent opposition.

The referral came primarily as a request for assistance by the staff to help them deal with the family and to sort out their feelings concerning how to proceed in the face of their frustrations. Included was a request for a consultation with the young man to discover if he was depressed and if anything could be done to help him make better use of his time. The medical situation was clearly articulated. There was partial improvement which had been arrested for some time. His life was safe for the moment but restricted to the hospital because of low resistance to infection and a possible bleeding disorder.

The stalemate with the illness resulted in the medical considerations receding into the background, with the consideration of the attitude toward the illness coming to the foreground. Concerns for this attitude became tinged increasingly with magical expectations. Even the medical staff started to wonder: if only the young man showed an unambivalent desire to get better, perhaps the graft versus host disease, and its many complications, would reverse itself.

In my assessment of the situation, the young man had made a compromise adaptation to a long debilitating hospitalization with frequent setbacks and continuing uncertainty. The inevitability of the final outcome was beginning to make itself felt. The possibilities for preparation, however, were closed off. Anticipatory grieving or any other sign of letting go suggested that a precipitous despair would unavoidably ensue. Everyone was feeling the desperation and looking to hold others to account for the lack or progress and resolution. There was an inability to bring the young man, his family, and the hospital to see themselves divided into factions in response to the same unanswerable struggle.

There are many ways to look at a situation such as this, each way providing its own interpretative framework. My suggestion is that we see it as a crisis of hope and articulate it as such. A dynamic psychology of hope will provide a clinically close and immediately relevant discussion of the issues apparent in the situation just described. Hope is often thought of and spoken of as a static concept. Like a traffic light, if hope is "on," one can press ahead; if hope is "off," either the brakes have been applied or the fuel has run out. As a static concept, hope is also dealt with as a token, as something that can be given or taken away. But hope is not a static thing; it is dynamic. The dynamic concept of hope is related to the feeling of loss and, in turn, to the sense of entitlement.

Starting with the dictionary definition, hope is the expectation of something desired. Loss is to feel a detriment resulting from deprivation. Entitlement is to have a sense of desert or just claim. These definitions, if applied to a serious illness, give rise to issues of hope and despair when one conceives of illness as a time trajectory. Time emphasizes the existential aspects. During a period of well-being the ultimate hope is an illusion of immortality. There is an unshaken sense of expectation in conjunction with a strong feeling of personal, particularly bodily, continuity. The feeling of bodily integrity allows for a direct sense of continuity without having to abstract cognitively into the future. On the other hand, expectation does reflect man's capacity for abstraction, which can be lost in profound hopelessness and its ensuing depression. For our dynamic psychology, hope is the conjunction of expectation and continuity.

The sense of entitlement can be considered normal or natural in the presumption of an average life expectancy, a statistical myth. Whatever uncertainty exists, it remains relatively distant and ignored. When a serious illness, such as cancer, strikes, one is ill for a variable period of time during which death is seen to approach or recede. There is an entitled future to be lost along with some presumptive expectations which may extend well beyond the recognition of any end point. The presumption of the normal entitlement is lost. The attempts to preserve the illusion of immortality are marred by the greater presence of uncertainty.

Hope strives to sustain the sense of expectation and continuity, to restore the illusion of immortality. The dialectic of shaken hope and changed entitlement is where the emotional precipitate of loss and deprivation is crystallized. The knowledge of loss readjusts the sense of entitlement. This conception of entitlement is best understood as a process of valuation from which the particular sense of entitlement arises. The wants of the individual are brought into a negotiated weighing with the provisions of reality. This necessity forces a cleavage between what is felt to be an imperative need and what can be relegated to the less pressing realm of desire, thus making for a readjustment in values and an adjustment to finitude. This calibration of entitlement determines the investment of value the individual places in living and thereby in the global attachment to life itself. The sense of entitlement may be exaggerated, or there may be a sense of nonentitlement. This will also be reflected in the nature of the hopes or their absence and in the response to loss. For in critical illness it appears that hope during the period of well-being is the psychological antidote to veiled uncertainty. With the dynamic realignment, as described above, hope is more poignantly felt as vulnerability. How that vulnerability is handled accounts for the two general patterns of disillusionment presented below.

This view pictures entitlement as a process determining the establishment of values, influencing the determination of hopes and thereby also influencing the response to losses. This conception of entitlement has its foundations in general theories of distributive shares as are found in other social sciences—law, ethics, political economy, etc. Therefore, it has a place as a bridging concept to these other sciences. It is a conception that is also consonant with George Kriegman's hypothesis of bimodal determination: social and psychological.

Looking back at the clinical situation, the loss of the normal entitlement was denied. No dynamic readjustment was acknowledged, giving rise to the necessity for false hope and thereby creating a web of barbed illusion. In doing so, false hope exploits the sense of entitlement. In this clinical vignette all those involved continually reiterated the same disillusionment. The recognition of mortality is a painful thing to contemplate. But it also provides a test of our resources to find hope where otherwise it may not seem discoverable, for example, through reexperiencing the awe of just being alive. People say there are many finite moments that are worth a lifetime. Had our young patient's family been able to adjust, perhaps they might have found an occasion to deepen and openly feel their love for one another.

Mortality is only one of the modifiers of entitlement and only one of many influences on the dynamics of hope. How can the dynamic concept of hope be generalized to show how people are matched to their circumstances? This can be seen in patterns of hope management. Let me describe two patterns of hope management arising in situations where the potential for disillusionment is a consideration.

The first pattern I call gradual disillusionment. Here the individual gradually absorbs, in bits and pieces so to speak, an unwelcome reality. It happens gradually because of the timing of successive events and is modified by the individual's ability to work it through. With this pattern of hope there is a successive approximation of the unpleasant truth by working through a psychological pain as a means to the restoration of hope. Unwelcome circumstances are faced squarely. Since there is always a danger of premature and precipitous abandonment of hope, this adaptation can go astray and result in misplaced emotions. In the oncology situation this is a common happening at the time of first reoccurence, which is not always as foreboding as it may appear.

The second general pattern of hope I call late disillusionment. Here the response to an unwelcome reality is almost imperceptible until an overwhelming recognition takes place. If the losses are great, there is a possibility of profound abandonment of hope, and despair takes its place. This pattern depends on the succession of events and on different individual capacities. With the overwhelming recognition, the capacity for working through can be overstretched by the emotional traumas or can in some other way become unequal to the task of adaptation. The loss of hope may be so severe that the ability to make restitution is also lost. Our clinical vignette was a case of late disillusionment. The truth made itself apparent even in the face of the hollow denials that did little to ease the air of crisis with its impending, sudden despair.

How do these two patterns of hope show how people are matched to their circumstances? The best clue will be given by a dynamic formulation of their hopes that pictures hope as relative to the sense of entitlement and conjointly relative to the feeling of loss. Hope, loss and entitlement are an inseparable, dynamic triad (Silberfeld, 1981).

Entitlement near the End of Life and Narcissism

This chapter began with recognizing the role mortality plays in attenuating man's narcissism. When faced with calamity, the response is frequently: Why me? To appreciate the contribution that the modification of entitlement at the end of life may make to our understanding of this question, it is instructive to stand it on its head: Why not me?

The recognition of mortality encourages an appreciation of personal finitude. The knowledge of personal finitude is accompanied by an adjustment of entitlement which must nevertheless permit each man his own uniqueness. Personal myths all come to the same end. And so personal pride has to find its place within the commonality of a shared fate. Pride only exists in the perspective of others, present or past. And so personal values take their place within the perennial values of mankind. How could an individual recognize his uniqueness other than by comparison within the human mainstream? Pride requires a recognition of others and a shared commonality of values. For pride to be just, it requires a reciprocity with the values of others.

A sense of continuity near the end of life is achieved by giving over hopes to those near us, most often to children. But continuity is also achieved by recognizing our fate as resting within the continuity of our community at large. The nuclear age forcefully presses this recognition upon us. It will or has caused a reevaluation of our sense of entitlement and a realignment of values. If we are to continue our perennial hopes into the future, we must not exaggerate our entitlement to exercise our considerable powers of knowledge.

Why not me? Because "why me?" is ineffable and has no answer in living experience. It is possible to be exceptional, but only in so far as one has received a gift from the Almighty. It is not possible to be exceptional by exaggerating or denying the sense of entitlement common to all. False pride comes from a rejection of one's humanity along with that of humanity at large. The capacity for true pride and empathy requires a sense of finitude and an acceptance of commonality. The readjustment of entitlement near the end of life reaffirms this, as it has throughout man's history. Perhaps this is the wisdom of our elders which we have forsaken in the cult of youth and in our culture of narcissism. The proximity to death brings a balanced sense of entitlement which too often waits a lifetime to be achieved.

REFERENCES

Becker, K. 1973. *The denial of death*. New York: Free Press.

Freud, S. 1915. Thoughts for the times on war and death. In *Standard edition*, 14:273–300. London: Hogarth Press, 1974.

Kriegman, G. 1983. Entitlement attitudes: Psychological and therapeutic implications. *J. Am. Acad. Psychoanal.* 11:265–81.

Silberfeld, M. 1981. Hope, loss, and entitlement: lessons from the oncology situation. *Can. J. Psychiatry* 26:415–18.

4.

The Psychology of Rights

Robert Michels

To a philosopher, a right is a claim that is justified. The individual who has a right may not be able to exercise it; he may be too weak, or inhibited, or others may be too powerful, evil, or corrupt for him to be successful in pursuing it. The individual may not even desire that to which he has a right—it may be burdensome or at least not much fun. But to say that he has a right is to say that he is justified if he does choose to pursue it.

The concept of rights, defined in this way, has more to do with law or ethics than with psychology. However, there are some important psychological dimensions to our understanding of rights. First, some rights have been said to exist because of the psychological needs of man. For example, Ribble (1965) has written of the "rights of infants," and in general the recognition that human beings require certain psychological substrates in order to survive, just as they require oxygen or food or warmth, has led to the recognition that a right to life implies a right to these psychological essentials for life.

However, there is a more complex relationship between rights and psychology. There is a subjective inner dimension to a right, the feeling and belief that one is entitled. Most often, as is common in psychological and psychoanalytic thinking, this is discussed in terms of its pathologic variants. An individual may feel entitled to things when most others would not agree—patients with narcissistic syndromes and Freud's (1916) and Jacobson's (1959) discussions of "exceptions" come to mind. On the other hand, an individual may not believe himself entitled in situations in which others generally agree he should be. Depressive (and some masochistic) syndromes are examples. These seemingly opposite conditions may coexist, alternate, or be layered, with one used as a defense against the other, as is common in syndromes that combine masochistic and narcissistic pathology. Finally, although I have used "feel" and "believe" interchangeably, and in most situations they are closely linked, this is not always the case. For example, an individual may believe himself to have rights that he does not feel that he possesses (mild depressive syndromes with diminished self-esteem come to mind) or may feel entitled to something although cognitively he would recognize that he is not (as is seen in some manic syndromes and is common in adolescence).

A sense of entitlement grows developmentally from early experiences of the attitudes of significant others, particularly parents, toward one's rights. Of course, parental attitudes toward their children's rights are closely related to their sense of their own rights and their security in them. Thus social groups that feel themselves to be disadvantaged may transmit anxiety about their rights to their children either in the form of defensive exaggeration of entitlement or, in an identification with the aggressor, as an acceptance of diminished entitlement. A similar psychodynamic constellation may occur when parents with pathological narcissism evoke in their children the exaggerated entitlement of the "exception," often in an attempt to compensate for what they perceive as some defect in the child. Many of the characteristic personality traits of individuals with serious defects from birth or early childhood stem not from the defect itself but rather from the effects of the parents' defensive response to the narcissistic wound that their child's defect represents.

In psychoanalysis and the psychoanalytic psychotherapies the most critical therapeutic issues regarding rights and entitlements are likely to emerge in the transference. The therapeutic situation is an asymmetric one. It is far more successful at protecting the therapist's rights than the patient's. Both metaphorically and actually the therapist sits in the most comfortable seat, controls the time and place of meetings, receives payment, and is protected from discomfort. This is essential if the treatment is to be successful, but it is easily perceived by the patient not only as a necessary aspect of a therapeutic arrangement but also as a recreation of childhood experiences in which one's own rights and entitlements were subordinated to those of others. Indeed, this perception of the therapeutic experience is in many ways the core of the transference, without which psychoanalytic treatments would be impossible. There are several ways in which patients respond to this perception. Perhaps the easiest to understand and manage is the patient who complains about the inequity and protests that the treatment has become part of the problem rather than part of the solution, and by so doing makes his transferential interpretation clear, vivid, and amenable to therapeutic inquiry and exploration. More difficult, as Kriegman (1983) has pointed out, is the patient who perceives the situation in the same way but accepts the experience without complaint, feeling his lack of entitlement as appropriate and expected, in effect as a confirmation of his view of himself as not having a justified claim to expect any more. This response is often misunderstood as a rational recognition of the appropriate needs of the therapeutic relationship, as a capacity to establish an unconflicted therapeutic alliance, when it actually represents a transferential misperception of the relationship concealed because of a hopelessness about the possibility of things ever being otherwise and a desire to avoid the painful arousal of long dormant wishes that cannot possibly be gratified.

The task of the therapist is first to create a setting in which there are no capricious or inappropriate insensitivities to the patient's rights and in which those rights are recognized, supported, and endorsed, while at the same time there is no attempt to placate or mollify the patient by gratifications that grow out of a desire to dilute the patient's resentment and disapppointment or bribe him into pseudocompliance. Second, after this setting has been created, the therapist must be sensitive to the patient's responses to it, accepting and tolerating anger or dissatisfaction and interpreting resistances to expressing, or even experiencing, the frustrations of the treatment. Third, after this has been accomplished and the patient's responses have been clarified and articulated, they can be related to his patterns of response in other life situations outside of therapy and, ultimately, to their genetic origins in experiences within the matrix of his original family.

This theme of rights, entitlements, and their exaggerations and inhibitions is not the only theme in psychoanalytic therapy, but it is an important one. It is elicited by the very form of the therapeutic relationship, and it is a common infrastructure to the specific dynamic themes of the various types of psychopathology. In effect, whatever specific wishes, fears, or defenses lie at the core of neurotic symptoms or character patterns, there are always additional psychological structures that have predisposed or developed secondarily to the pathology, and that are important in maintaining it. Masochistic and narcissistic structures, along with disturbances in the area of rights and entitlements, are prominent in this role.

The concepts of rights and entitlements also help to elucidate some types of "acting out" of transferences that can occur in psychotherapy. Patients who have an inhibited or constricted sense of their rights may be helped by psychotherapy. They become aware of wishes they had long deferred or denied. Often this is accompanied by a strong positive transference, a feeling that at last they have found a parent figure who recognizes and supports what earlier parents had rejected. Pursuing one's rights becomes more than simply recognizing entitlements that had been put aside; it is also pleasing a therapist who is encouraging their recognition. The recognition of what had in the past been deferred creates a variant of the "exception" situation. The individual is not only entitled to his current entitlements, he is entitled to more because of what he had so long denied himself. The consequence of these dynamics is that the patient who had long felt pathologically underentitled may, in treatment, pass through a phase of exaggerated entitlement. This is a psychological parallel to the well-known social phenomenon of the consequences of a long underprivileged group developing rising expectations that lead to angry demands and strong feelings of entitlement in response to the beginning recognition of their long denied rights.

Some of these themes can be illustrated by the discussion of a patient. A forty-five-year-old, married, successful attorney sought consultation somewhat reluctantly on the advice of a close personal friend. They had been jogging together, and the patient had revealed that he was thinking of leaving his wife of twenty years. The friend, who knew them both, told him that he should see a psychiatrist before doing anything so impulsive and out of character. He came expecting me to try to talk him out of his plan. He described his wife as a wonderful person, intelligent, attractive, devoted to their marriage, and a devoted mother to their children. One of these was an attractive and successful adolescent boy; the other was a younger girl who had had some psychological problems—school phobias and mild anorectic symptoms. He was quite successful at his practice, although he was aware that others perceived him as arrogant and insensitive in personal relationships.

The immediate situation had started a few weeks before when he was taking a train home from a bar association meeting. He found that he was sitting next to an attractive young woman whom he had previously met. They began to talk, and he found a feeling of resonance and understanding that he had not known since the beginning of his marriage. Within a few days they began an affair, and the relationship had deepened since that time. He had known this feeling only once before, as an adolescent when he had an intense infatuation with a girl from a lower status ethnic background to whom his family objected. Shortly after they started to date, his father had suddenly died. He broke off the relationship with the girl rather than distress his grieving mother further. Within a year he married his wife, a member of his family's social group and in the eyes of his family a thoroughly acceptable choice. He had never felt the peak of passion or excitement with his wife that he had experienced with the other girl, and for the first few years of the marriage often thought of what he had given up. However, he felt that he was not entitled to complain; he was married to a personable and attractive woman and was successful in his professional world. He felt guilty about his flight from marriage to his career, and even more about his occasional, brief flirtations with other women. His wife was sexually compliant but little more. She generally acted as though sex was his right (and her duty), a view he shared.

His past history provided some interesting insight into his readiness to subordinate his own wishes to the needs of others. He was the youngest of four children. His older brother was congenitally blind; his mother devoted herself to ensuring that, in spite of this, his brother received every possible advantage in education and socialization. The patient had only the dimmest memories of competition or envy, although he did recall his fear and later anger at his brother's violent tantrums. He was a quiet adolescent, in retrospect depressed, but he never viewed it that way. His life changed when he went to college. He felt liberated, poured himself into his work, his friendships, and the sense of freedom he discovered living away from home. He felt guilty that his first infatuation was with a girl whom he knew would be rejected by his family, but he was young, and although his feelings were intense, there was no thought of permanence. Then disaster had struck in the form of his father's sudden death, his family's crisis, and his decision to return home, take over his father's business, and support and protect his mother and his less competent although older siblings.

In effect, he had learned to suppress any feelings of entitlement as a child, and then when they had emerged briefly in adolescence, fate had provided a powerful reminder that he should never have strayed from his original path. The immediate situation had developed in the context of his daughter's reaching adolescence and responding to her puritanical mother with an exaggerated asceticism that suggested to him that his children would continue the self-denials and frustrations that had marked his own life. He finally rebelled.

The past seemed to explain the present, but another aspect of the picture emerged in the transference. He was quite affluent and was accustomed to purchasing expert advice and then having it available when and where he wanted it. He was entitled only to what he could afford, but when he could afford it, this entitlement extended to behavior that could be rude and insensitive. His self-denial, coupled with an almost compulsive generosity, meant that he had paid his dues, and the desires that he suppressed and controlled so much of the time emerged with a vengeance when he released them. When wishes are embedded in conflict, their denial and suppression is usually only part of the clinical picture that results.

Two episodes, one in his life, the other in the treatment, illustrate the conflict. The first occurred about a year after I first saw him. He separated from his wife, and there was acrimonious conflict over the financial arrangements. He won, felt victorious, and then a few months later gave her a gift that was more than the amount that had been contested. She accepted it but did not express any gratitude, and he was angry and depressed.

The second had to do with the arrangements for our appointments. I saw him four times a week. Three of our appointments were at times convenient for him, at the end of his professional day. The fourth was not, and he complained about it, although I never had the feeling that the complaints were coupled with any expectation that I would change the schedule. Then he arranged to be appointed to the board of an important local charity that met at the time of this fourth appointment. When he told me about this he was obviously astonished that I still did not plan to change the time. He was no longer asking for anything for himself, but rather he himself was making a sacrifice for others. A critical issue in the treatment revolved around my pointing out that I considered his own desire an equally valid basis for his request; ironically, to have acceded to his second request would have been to agree with his own view of how insignificant were his personal wishes. For a period of time after we explored this question he decided that he did not really want either to see me or to go to the board meetings (although when I pointed out that it had not occurred to him that he might also "play hooky" from work, he at first had difficulty even understanding my suggestion).

How does the concept of entitlement enhance our understanding of this kind of data? Psychoanalytic theory initially focused on wishes and drives, the motivational roots of behavior. The ubiquitousness of psychic conflict and the many varieties of disguises, transformations, and defenses against wishes soon led to a second focus on the forces that counter forbidden wishes, patterns of defense and unconscious fantasies of imagined danger that stem from the earliest years of development. Together with the signal affects of anxiety and depression, these concepts offered a scheme for exploring psychic conflict: wish, danger, anxiety, defense, and compromise formation. However, the scheme was only a skeleton, and it called attention to the need for flesh, a context or frame in which the conflict occurred. Concepts such as ego, character, and self have provided this context. With them, there had been an expansion of psychoanalytic interest beyond the elements of psychic conflict that were adequate to explain specific symptoms so that it encompassed other features of mental life as well. Entitlement can be understood as an aspect of this broader context, as one pattern of the ego's attitude toward and adaptation to a wish. In this regard it is similar to narcissistic or masochistic attitudes, and like them can be a major factor in determining the inaccessibility of a segment of the personality to therapeutic intervention. If a masochistic person feels that he ought to suffer, if a narcissistic person believes that what others view as his problem is actually something that makes him special, or if a patient feels he is not entitled to have his wishes fulfilled, then an approach to treatment that ignores these issues and simply addresses the core conflict between wish and fear will be experienced by the patient more as an intrusion than as an opportunity for growth and change.

In addition to the social, ethical, and legal meaning of rights, we must recognize a psychological dimension: entitlement or the attitude toward one's desires. These attitudes are shaped by early experience, particularly by the internalization of the attitudes of significant others. They may be pathologically diminished or exaggerated or, as is common in mental conflict, may be marked by a mixture of these extremes. They are an important theme of psychotherapy, stimulated in part by the inevitable frustrations and asymmetries of the therapeutic situation. As psychoanalysis broadened its interest from the basic framework of psychic conflict to the complex nuances of the human condition, issues of entitlement have received greater attention as critical determinants of psychopathology and limiting factors determining the potential impact of psychotherapy.

REFERENCES

Freud, S. 1916. Some character-types met with in psychoanalytic work. In *Standard edition*, 14:311–15. London: Hogarth Press, 1957.

Jacobson, E. 1959. The "exceptions": An elaboration of Freud's character study. In *The psychoanalytic study of the child*, 14:135–54. New York: International Universities Press.

Kriegman, G. 1983. Entitlement attitudes: Psychosocial and therapeutic implications. *J. Am. Acad. Psychoanal.* 11:365–81.

Ribble, M. 1965. *The rights of infants: Early psychological needs and their satisfaction.* 2d ed. New York: Columbia University Press.

5·

Envy, the Most Painful Affect:

Its Relation to Entitlement

and Helplessness

Cecil C. H. Cullander

A LETTER to Andrei Petrovich:

> You took me out of the cold, you took me under your wing. . . .
> you took pity on me, gathered up a drunk. You put me between
> linen sheets. The material was so smooth and cool; it was calcu-
> lated to soothe my anger and ease my anxiety. It did.
> . . . . . I had a bed
> . . . . . You gave me a bed
> From the height of your well-being, you lowered a cloud-bed,
> a halo that surrounded me with magic warmth, wrapped me in
> memories, nostalgia without bitterness, and hopes. It seemed I
> could still have much of what was intended for me in my youth.
> You are my benefactor, Andrei Petrovich!

63

...I want to convey my feelings to you.
Strictly speaking, it's all one feeling: hatred.
I hate you.
I'm writing this letter to bring you down a peg.
From my first day with you I felt afraid.
You stifled me.
You crushed me under your weight.
.... Who gave you the right to crush me?
How am I worse than you?
Are you more intelligent?
Are you richer spiritually?
Are you on a higher level of organization?
Stronger? More important?
Superior not only in position, but in essence?
Why must I acknowledge your superiority? [38–39]

Thus is described, by the author Yuri Olesha (1981) in a story called "Envy," the experience of extreme envy—with the components of entitlement, the helpless feeling of the other's superiority in his very essence, hatred, and, in the story, the eventual "revenge" against and destruction of the benevolent object.

Many authors have made references to or described envy in its various vicissitudes. Richard III displayed not only extreme envy but jealousy and vengefulness. Freud (1916) has given extensive discussion of the dynamics of Macbeth and his lady: their childlessness and envy of their benevolent leader, Duncan. Freud (1900) in the analysis of one of his own dreams also cites his painful awareness of envy of his son's youth and the wish for the son's death! A glance at the index of *The Great Treasury of Western Thought* lists twenty-two entries on envy, including Plutarch, Euripides, Epictetus, Pope, Freud, Tocqueville, and Joyce but, curiously, not the Bible or Samuel Johnson. Envy is one of the deadly sins, and in Proverbs 27:4 it is stated, "Wrath is cruel and anger is outrageous, but who is able to stand before envy?" (Rodgers, 1982).

Samuel Johnson, as reported by his biographer W. Jackson Bate (1979), was much concerned with envy and its impact on human relations:

> Envy is of all vices closest to "pure and unmixed evil" because its object is "lessening others, though we gain nothing to ourselves." To this extent, it violates "the great law of human benevolence" more than "self-interest" does. . . . the real motivation in "the cold malignity of envy" is "not so much its own happiness as another's misery." The young Rasselas cannot believe that a man would wish to "injure another without benefit to himself." "Pride is seldom delicate, it will please itself with very mean advantages; and envy feels not its own happiness, but when it may be compared with the misery of others." In professional as well as social life Johnson notes how envy contributes to the cult of mediocrity, smoothing the path for those who make us better "pleased with ourselves." The acrimony of literary critics is often excited merely by "hearing applauses which another enjoys": the palm of popularity in drawing rooms goes to persons whose conversation is "unenvied insipidity." Envy is naturally all the greater in professions where performance cannot be objectively measured, and where the main external reward is (or thought to be) that most elusive of things, "reputation." [308–9]

We see from such writings that envy is an ingredient of the human condition. In various papers the utility of normal envy in the natural development of the child is commented upon. However, without presenting an exhaustive exegesis of the concept I want to offer definitions and distinctions—particularly with regard to jealousy. The *Oxford English Dictionary* defines envy: "The feeling of mortification and ill-will occasioned by the contemplation of superior advantages possessed by another. To feel displeasure and ill-will at the superiority of [another person] in happiness, success, reputation, or the possession of anything desirable." For jealousy, its definition is: "[to be] troubled by the belief, suspicion or fear that the good [in relation to another] which one desires to gain or keep for oneself has been or may be diverted to another." Henry Stack Sullivan (1956) simply states, in interpersonal terms, "Envy is an acute discomfort caused by discovering that somebody else has something that one feels one *ought* to have" (129; my italics, relating to the concept of entitlement). Thus envy is distinguished as a two-party phenomenon. Jealousy as defined by Sullivan is much like the *OED* definition but in interpersonal terms more succinctly stated as a three-party event.

Clearly, it is understood that the three-party event of the jealousy dynamic is the oedipal triangle, as well as, oftentimes, the contributions of sibling rivalry.

Review of Contributions

In recent years there have been several papers dealing with the concept of envy (Joffe 1969, Spielman 1971, Frankel and Sherick 1977, Begoin and Begoin 1979, Neubauer 1982, Rodgers 1982). These papers reflect the increased interest in envy and present contributions from workers in the direct observation of infants and children, in mother-infant, parent-child settings. Much of such observation comes from colleagues at the various child study centers (Hampstead, Yale, Michigan).

Melanie Klein (1957) asserted that "I consider envy an oral-sadistic and anal-sadistic expression of destructive impulses, operative from the beginning of life, and that it has a constitutional basis" (ix). An earlier analyst, Eisler 1922, stated: "Envy in particular seems to me to be always a narcissistic sidestream arising out of the oral instinct, and is an important clue towards establishing a character based on this component instinct. Wherever it is possible to observe envy at an early stage, in children, for instance [note he says children, not newborns or infants] we find that it is directed only against people to whom there is simultaneously a libidinal attachment" (30–42). This earlier author specifies an important aspect of envy which is also stated by later workers, that is, that "there is simultaneously a libidinal attachment," and thereon hangs our therapeutic hope.

Whereas Klein and her school consider envy an inborn, constitutional given, other workers consider the development of envy dependent upon self-object differentiation with the accompanying development of intentionality. That is, envy is not, in their view, an expression of constitutional destructive impulses. Several authors believe that early distortions in self-esteem regulation are relative to the infant-mother unit and can stimulate excesses of aggression being turned toward the self and leading to self-destructive and masochistic predispositions associated with omnipotent fantasies that cannot be realized. Cooper (1983) comments on this in his discussion of the "Unusually Painful Analysis." He says these persons present a "sense of deadened capacity to feel, muted pleasure, a hyper-sensitive self-esteem alternating between grandiosity and humiliation, and inability to sustain or derive satisfaction from their relationships or their work, a constant sense of *envy*, an unshakable conviction of being wronged and deprived by those who are *supposed* to care for them and an infinite capacity for provocation and self-damage." He speculates that the origin of such a condition and affect state lies in the early developmental lines before separation and individuation, which are perforce painful, as are many aspects of growing into self-hood. It is the mother-infant unit which is faulty—again the statements refer to inadequate mothering and failure to accept pain as part of normal development.

Kohut (1972) discusses what he calls "narcissistic rage." In his system such rage arises early in the vulnerable person wherein archaic aggressions seek to establish control over a narcissistically experienced world. The genetic factors are those postulated for the narcissistic personality; that is, the failure of the unempathic mother in facilitating the infant's developing ego in acknowledgment of the inherent limitations of the power of the grandoise self. Such an ego attributes its failure and weakness to the malevolence and corruption of the uncooperative object. Such a circumstance leads, in the extreme, to "chronic narcissistic rage—one of the most pernicious afflictions of the human psyche—either, in its still endogenous and preliminary form, as grudge and spite, or externalized and acted out, in disconnected vengeful acts or in a cunningly plotted vendetta" (396–97). Such is portrayed in the opening passage of the story *Envy* by Yuri Olesha.

Olinick (1964), in his seminal paper on the negative therapeutic reaction, described the reaction of the patient to an economically and structurally correct interpretation:

(a) The reaction is paradoxically negativistic, in that it refuses, repudiates, and renounces inappropriately to the external situation. *The negativism is directed not so much at the issues raised by the confrontation or interpretation as at the person of the confronter or interpreter in an intensification of the transference.* [Italics added.]

(b) This transference is *overtly negative and hostile, but it is latently or unconsciously positive.* It is the pressure of the drives and affects encompassed by the positive transference that arouses the sequence of defensive rejection, self-punishment by symptom-excerbation, and alloplastic attack upon the therapist.

(c) The general orientation is sadomasochistic, and resistance arises from the superego.

(d) Out of this matrix there develops the dramatic, alloplastic intent. It is not only that the patient projects on to the analyst, but he also *vigorously attempts to mould the analyst into the very prototype of the hated yet beloved introject. The transferred impulses and affects are* ambivalent, pregenital, and intense.

(e) There is, finally, an uncanniness about these reactions, which I believe to be related to the resonant affects and impulses in the analyst induced by the patient's profound narcissistic conviction that his very existence depends on his ability to transform reality in accord with his infantile omnipotence. [121–22]

Olinick also is of the view that there is an underlying depression in such patients, which is "dreaded as death or destruction: the world will be empty, and they will be abandoned, drained and alone," as well as a "dread of regression," which is feared as "a loss of intactness, or annihilation of self, and is defended against by negativism. I would further propose that this dreaded *helplessness* and emotional surrender is inherent in the ambivalent identification with a depressed, pre-oedipal maternal love object" (121).

Here, also, is agreement with Eisler's (1922) view as to the simultaneous presence of not only hostile, destructive drive but also a "libidinal" attachment. Olinick summarizes his view of the life of these persons: "the recurrent pattern of living of those prone to the negative therapeutic reaction is of intolerance of gratification. At its height, the depressive, sado-masochistic rage is projected and often induced in the other person. Defences are directed against expected inner loss and helpless [*sic*] regression to the primary identifications with the depressed mother. Schematically, sadomasochism 'projects' depression, and negativism 'rejects' depression" (121; see also Cooper, 1983).

Valenstein (1973), also addressing the problem of negative therapeutic reaction, theorizes "in the development of such individuals, instead of the early pleasurable object experiences being consolidated into love and a sense of trust, the opposite occurs. Early affects are predominantly painful and as such recur consistently, crystallizing in the direction of attachment to pain and distrust of objects" (389). This occurs preverbally and pregenitally and hence is primarily operative in the oral, then anal and phallic periods. Such persons are beset by pathological envy directed most emphatically toward those who are/were expected to give love and care. They experience their envy with great pain and helplessness and yet, because of their exaggerated entitlement, are strongly attached to its presence.

To summarize the issues of agreement among the various workers quoted:

1. The origin of pathological envy is at the level of the mother-infant unit developmentally.

2. It is characterized by an ambivalent positive-negative attachment to a "not so good" (Winnicott 1965) mother.

3. There is a dread of regression, which is perceived as a state of utter helplessness.

4. There is marked difficulty in the oral, anal, and phallic phases relating to omnipotence, exaggerated entitlement, and a failure to develop the capacity to tolerate the pain of existence, particularly noted in the separation-individuation phase.

5. There is strong suggestion that there is early attachment to painful object-relatedness and an "infinite capacity for provocation" (Cooper) of painful experience and feeling wronged.

The Most Painful Affect

Before proceeding to a discussion of a therapeutic approach to those persons centrally afflicted with pathological envy, I want to state why I assert that envy is the most painful affect. I repeat the *Oxford English Dictionary* definition of envy, with some modification: "The feeling of *mortification*[1] and ill-will occasioned by the contemplation of superior advantages possessed by another [and which advantages have to do with internal possessions, which the envier feels *entitled* to and unfairly denied]" (italics added). Envy is most painful since it is also directed toward one to whom there is strong positive attachment. They are people who could be (and are ambivalently) admired, even emulated. There also can be the feeling of gratitude directed toward the envied person (Klein 1957). To be envied is also a most painful circum-

1. From *Oxford English Dictionary*: "Deadening or destruction of vital or active qualities; or impoverished—by the existence of desirable attributes possessed by someone who could be admired, but is hated. These attributes the envious one feels *entitled* to, but cheated of."

stance (Rodgers 1982) when the person who is being envied possesses various admirable attributes, including love for the envying person. As Johnson has observed, the fear of being envied leads to "unenvied insipidity" (Bate 1979). Rodgers also remarks on this in her paper on "Women and the Fear of Being Envied." Envy cannot be rationalized as readily as other closely related affects:

Jealousy: the jealous one can claim unfair treatment by the two persons who "exclude" him or her.

Hate: there always can be a rationale for hating someone.

Anger: here, also, one can "explain" one's anger.

Grief: a deeply painful affect, yet it can be assuaged with the acceptance of loss and through the sympathy of others.

But envy confronts one with a deep and helpless sense of being empty. Begoin and Begoin (1979), in a case report, express their view that severe envy is a quality of catastrophic anxiety in which the necessary object is "out of reach. . . . the subject [patient] is lost physically, by the object. . . . like the child whose parents had 'forgotten' him at school . . . the lost child [severely envious person] feels like a person who desperately attempts to hang on to a completely smooth surface on which there is no grip at all" (13). The capacity of some of these severely envious people to dramatically describe their plight can call forth a useful empathy in the therapist, thereby making possible or enhancing the therapeutic process.

Treatment Prospects

Pathological envy has not been presented as a clinical entity in and of itself but rather as a severely painful—most painful—affect which is central to what is nosologically identified as pathological narcissism and borderline character disorder. There is a close resemblance in the dynamics and origins of pathological envy to conditions distinguished as negative therapeutic reaction, chronic narcissistic rage, and masochistic-narcissistic character structure. The factors discussed above in relation to the origins of pathological envy contribute to the qualities that must be considered in a therapeutic approach:

1. The severe regression and dependence which develops and for which one must be prepared, as Winnicott (1965) cautions.

2. In all of the authors cited, and in my own experience, comment is made about the patient's extreme sensitivity to failures of empathy on the therapist's part and their own faulty capacity for empathy.

3. Intolerance of abstinence and "analytic neutrality" as we generally employ them. This posture is interpreted as the therapist's not caring.

4. Intolerance of separation: weekend, holiday, in short the therapist's absence for any reason.

5. Extreme sensitivity to interpretations and clarifications which are, in the main, experienced as rebuke.

6. Wide fluctuations in self-esteem—from omnipotent grandiosity and exaggerated entitlement to deadness, unworthiness, and helplessness.

7. Profound attacks on the therapist's self-esteem, his therapeutic zeal, and his very being.

So, how may we treat these impossible, suffering people by means of our impossible profession? Olinick (1964) says: "For work with these patients, it is essential that the analyst has a capacity for emphatic identification in a context of having worked through his own projective distortions and sadomasochistic defences, and has developed his own realistic sense of the relativity of values. . . . the approach is throughout intended to establish within the patient a new set of introjects that are less hateful and hated than those already present." These are ideal hopes and expectations of oneself, but who among us has so thoroughly worked through the vicissitudes of one's humanness? He softens this perfect stance with the statement that the analyst's angry assertiveness, if it is tactfully motivated and timed, is indicated and intended as the setting of limits. Joffe (1969) remarks that only negative responses are attained by the direct confrontation of envy. Instead, in his experience, "work on the patient's anxieties, together with realization of latent potential and unfulfilled ambition" (533) can lead to creativity and, in essence, a deep recognition on the patient's part of his positive inner contents (the emergence of the True Self, in Winnicott's terms) and that he is not empty. Other workers agree that in the circumstances of strong positive transference, envy can be identified if, also, the possibility of admiration is introduced. Cooper (1983) states that if the narcissistic side is interpreted, the masochistic side comes forth as defense, and vice versa. Terman (1975) gives perhaps the most precise description of his therapeutic approach. He outlines Kohut's view: "one cannot address oneself to the rage [envy] per se, but must deal with the archaic narcissistic matrix out of which it arises. That is, one must try to understand the way in which the archaic self is again damaged and in what the original damage consisted; then there will be a shift of such aggression in the service of realistic ambition" (241). He states further: "Neither education, the attempt to enlighten the individual so afflicted about the needs of others, nor the attempt to enlist the patient's momentarily detached observation is effective; the rage is only inflamed. In time the individual's capacity for empathy for potential offenders may be a more certain sign of integration and repair of the damaged self than simply the eradication of all such tantrums" (241). That is, an intellectual, exhortative, manipulative, explanatory, and suggestive approach is doomed to failure; only a deeply exploratory, steadfast, empathic technique can effect structural change. If the therapist is able to adhere to this formulation with conviction, he will have less tendency to become angry and to wish to withdraw from such patients. Because the therapist is not a perfectly empathic, understanding, and healing creature, failures are bound to occur; misunderstanding of the patient's envious, rageful attacks will further enrage the patient. Explanations are rejected; they are viewed as avoidance on the therapist's part to admit the patient's correctness. Terman recognizes that oftentimes the patient's attacks on the therapist are not of whole cloth but contain his perception of the therapist's character. If the therapist can, without abject distress, admit to error and defensiveness, the rage and envy may lessen or subside. But, also, the attack may totally dismantle the therapist. In such circumstance the therapist suffers assaults on his self-esteem and his worthiness as a therapist, even as a human being. It is at this edge that our saving grace may be that we recognize our empathic operation at its fullest—how the helpless child felt in the presence of overwhelming blows to its self-esteem. With steadfast persistence and the experience of a number of such encounters with the patient, the self becomes less vulnerable, and the patient is able to accept the defects of the therapist. Such a patient, after an extensive harangue at me, delineating, quite accurately, my defects and stubbornness, stopped, smiled and said, "My god, I'm like my father! I damn you if you do, and I damn you if you don't." Of course this was not the end of such ripping sessions, but there began a gradually increasing growth of empathy, accompanied by an appreciation of his own creative capacity in the use of words and metaphor in the course of the fits he would "pitch." His use of language had something of the rhetoric of Dylan Thomas and Thomas Wolfe (once described as "Southern rhetoric on a rampage").

Clinical Example

Early in her treatment a twenty-seven-year-old unmarried, depressed woman recognized that her feelings of distance and uninvolvement with other people were closely related to her fears of being engulfed in helplessness if she allowed herself to become closer. This awareness occurred after a visit from her mother during which the patient felt attempts at incorporation on her mother's part. In restaurants the mother waited until the patient ordered and then ordered the same food; she shopped with the patient and also selected the same clothing and hair styling. This was experienced by the patient as invasive and consuming of her identity. Subsequent to this seemingly sudden awareness, the patient recalled clearly the long-standing two-way competition between her mother and herself. There was a mutual envy between the two. The patient was the eldest of three daughters, born one and a half and six years apart. The middle daughter was a compliant and easy child and favored by the mother. The patient had been a resistant, unrewarding infant and child and had proved to be a severe test of the mother's first mothering experience. Many memories were recovered dealing with the entitlement that the patient felt toward her mother and the extreme opposition the patient put to her mother's attempts to feed and comfort her. The patient vividly recalled her envy of her mother's ability to satisfy the second daughter's needs. She also felt jealousy and cheated entitlement with regard to the sister-mother relationship; however; her strongest feelings had to do with envy of the mother's capacity to care for the sister. When the third daughter was born, when the patient was eight and a half, she undertook to be a better mother to this sister than the mother was. She was, over the course of time, allowed to mother this sister and did so in a way which the mother grew to envy. This interaction became clearer during treatment at the time of the mother's visit referred to above and with subsequent visits and the recovery of memories. The mother's envy of the patient's youth, beauty, and skills was manifested in her attempts to so totally identify with the patient and thereby consume her. It was as if two persons could not exist independently. The coming into consciousness of these dynamics allowed the patient to become increasingly aware of their operation with people at her office and in social situations. She saw that her intense envy of the skills and attributes of others, to which she felt entitled, rendered her helpless in her wishes for intimacy. This mode came into the transference with full force. The patient envied the therapist's interpretative skill and empathy so intensely that she would refuse to talk, though coming each day to her appointments, lying on the couch with entitlement incarnate. She lay in wait for the therapist to make some error or to be late or inattentive. At such times she would pounce upon the discrepancy and enlarge it to a total character assassination. If the therapist responded with apparently correct interpretations, the patient accused him of patronizing her. It was only after many such skirmishes that the patient responded to the therapist's steadfast attendance to the task of analysis with empathy for the patient's suffering that there was a gradual lifting of the envious antagonism. A sense of admiration emerged—the patient for the therapist's skill and the therapist for the patient's determination to attend to the analytic work through all of the turmoil. As the work progressed, the patient developed a scornful pity for her mother—which then slowly shifted to a sense of sadness at her mother's failure to be a good enough mother to her. Eventually the patient felt remorse at her treatment of her mother over the years and no longer felt threatened by her mother's attempts to be like her. She was able to accept her mother as she was and felt no great stress at her mother's envy.

Conclusion

These people are among the most difficult to work with, as Cooper (1983) says in "The Unusually Painful Analysis"; yet they oftentimes are among the most rewarding to work with. Frequently they come from a background of parents who were brilliant, productive persons who contributed to their community and culture, but who failed in the all-important role of effective parent. Once freed from the majority of his envy and hurt, the patient is able to appreciate the contributions of the parent(s) and experience the grief of their failures in human relatedness. As we well know, not always are we successful in the treatment of such people; however, with the careful selection of cases we can hope for mutual rewards in our attempts.

REFERENCES

Adler, J., and C. Van Doren. 1977. *Great treasury of western thought.* New York: R. R. Bowker.

Bate, W. 1979. *Samuel Johnson.* New York: First Harvest/Harcourt Brace Jovanovich.

Begoin, J. and F. Begoin. 1979. Envy and catastrophic anxiety. Paper read at the 3d conference of the European Psycho-Analytic Federation, October 11–14, London.

Cooper, A. M. 1983. Masochistic-narcissistic characters and the unusually painful analysis. Paper read at the Annual Meeting of the Virginia Psychoanalytic Society, June 17–18, Norfolk.

Eisler, M. J. 1922. Pleasure in sleep and the disturbed capacity for sleep. *Int. J. Psycho-Anal.* 3:30–42.

Frankel, S., and I. Sherick. 1977. Observations on the development of normal envy. In *The psychoanalytic study of the child,* 32:257. New York: International Universities Press.

Freud, S. 1900. The interpretation of dreams. In *Standard edition,* 5:558–60. London: Hogarth Press, 1953.

———. 1916. Some character types met with in psycho-analytic work. In *Standard edition,* 14:309–33. London: Hogarth Press, 1957.

Jaffe, D. S. 1968. The masculine envy of woman's procreation function. *J. Am. Psychoanal. Assn.* 16:521–48.

Joffe, W. G. 1969. A critical review of the status of the envy concept. *Int. J. Psycho-Anal.* 50:533–45.

Klein, M. 1957. *Envy and gratitude.* New York: Basic Books.

Kohut, H. 1972. Thoughts on narcissism and narcissistic rage. In *The psychoanalytic study of the child,* 27:360–400. New York: International Universities Press.

Kriegman, G. 1983. Entitlement attitudes: Psychosocial and therapeutic implications. *J. Am. Acad. Psychoanal.* 11:265–81.

La Planche, J., and J. R. Pontalis. 1973. *The language of psychoanalysis.* New York: W. W. Norton.

Neubauer, P. B. 1982. Rivalry, envy, and jealousy. In *The psychoanalytic study of the child,* 37:121–41. New York: International Universities Press.

Olesha, Y. 1981. *Envy and other works.* Tr. R. Andrew MacAndrew. New York: W. W. Norton.

Olinick, S. L. 1964. The negative therapeutic reactions. *Int. J. Psycho-Anal.* 45:540–48.

Rodgers, J. A. 1982. Women and the fear of being envied. *Nursing Outlook* 30:344–47.

Spielman, P. M. 1971. Envy and jealousy: An attempt at clarification, *Psychoanal. Quart.* 40:59–82.

Sullivan, H. S. 1956. *Clinical studies in psychiatry.* New York: W. W. Norton.

Terman, D. M. 1975. Aggression and narcissistic rage: A clinical elaboration. *Annual of Psychoanal.,* 3:29–55. New York: International Universities Press.

Valenstein, A. F. 1973. On attachment to painful feelings and the negative therapeutic reaction. In *The psychoanalytic study of the child,* 28:365–92. New York: International Universities Press.

Winnicott, D. W. 1965. Ego distortion in terms of true and false self. In *The maturational processes and the facilitating environment.* New York: International Universities Press.

6.

Kriegman's "Nonentitlement" and Ibsen's *Rosmersholm*

D. Wilfred Abse

GEORGE KRIEGMAN (1983) has elaborated on the theme that attitudes of exaggerated entitlement or nonentitlement are often major factors in the individual's orientation to the world and an important aspect of his or her sense of identity. A stark example of an attitude of nonentitlement cropped up recently in my practice. A patient who twenty-five years ago suffered a prolonged, severe, florid schizophrenic illness, spent a period in the hospital and has since been maintained in regular outpatient psychotherapy. For several years he was treated by a psychoanalyst in a metropolitan center in an analytically oriented psychotherapy three times a week. About twenty years ago, he came under my care on a once weekly basis and has been able to stay out of the hospital, though unable to work and limited in his personal relationships. A World War II veteran, the patient has received regular benefits from the Veterans Administration and more recently from the

Social Security agency. Still more recently, his aged aunt died and left him a substantial legacy. Soon the patient wrote letters to government agencies disclaiming his benefits, thus arousing considerable bureaucratic turmoil and perplexity and anger in his relatives. In his letters to the agencies the patient expressed his view that he was not entitled to benefits and begged not to be prosecuted for fraud. Discussions later revealed that he felt that the authorities were planning to put him on trial for criminal fraudulence. He believed that various people in his community had reported him to the authorities and were making strange signs to warn him to get away from them. He wondered whether he should elect to become a fugitive from justice. These paranoid developments were accompanied by occasional hallucinosis, including accusatory voices. He insisted that he had not intended to commit a felony and sought my help to persuade the authorities that he made mistakes from time to time due to his confusion. He sought extenuation of his crime on the basis of his mental illness and hoped that I would testify on his behalf at his trial.

Actually this was a recrudescence of feelings of unworthiness and nonentitlement that had surfaced during his psychotherapy with me about fifteen years ago. At that time, the events that preceded his coming to the notice of the military authorities on account of mental illness were clarified. During the battle on Luzon, he was with several soldiers with machine guns holding a position on a hill. The gunners were running out of ammunition. The sergeant called for a volunteer to descend the hill, take a small boat on the foreshore to a hidden ship nearby where ammunition was stored, and bring it back. No one volunteered. The sergeant then called the patient's name, whereupon he left immediately even though the Japanese were bombing the bay and there was enemy fire on the way down. The patient succeeded in his mission, which required several descents and ascents, and later was suitably awarded a medal. More adequate anamnesis revealed that at the time the patient was already in a massively withdrawn state of mind, characterized by automatic obedience to the sergeant, and quite incapable of making a decision on an autodirectional level. He had become withdrawn earlier after witnessing the soldiers' activities with women of the island. Horror-stricken, he had been unable either to protest or to participate. During this phase of psychotherapy, he explained his behavior as really not meriting the commendation, in view of his confused mental state during which he had no appreciation of any danger from the enemy and was engaged heavily in erotic fantasies concerning girls he had felt afraid to approach in high school.

Such a psychotic, Kafkaesque instance indicates clearly that there are delusions of nonentitlement going beyond doubts and feelings into the realm of well-nigh absolute conviction. More usually, in neurosis, the inhibitions, the absence of predictable interest or behavior, lead to the uncovering of repressed notions and feelings of nonentitlement. Thus a patient in analysis may show over months, or even years, no evident curiosity about his or her analyst. In such instances, in my experience, the working through of feelings concerned with prohibitions in childhood against inquiry into the parents' secret conjugal activities results in a change of attitude about the analyst's private life. The unconscious prohibition is thus succeeded by felt frustration. Between these two poles of delusion and unawareness are the many instances of acknowledgment and disavowal of feelings of lack of entitlement encompassed by a split in the ego. Even more frequent is the alternation of exaggerated entitlement and nonentitlement attitudes, one the counterpoint of the other in the same neurotic individual.

Another type of exaggerated entitlement and nonentitlement may be represented in two bodies, as a common type of marital incompatibility. Levin (1969) has pointed out that some women feel they have a right to avoid sexual relations with their husbands whenever they wish and that the husbands should nonetheless always love and admire them and not react unfavorably to such avoidance. Levin shows that a husband's depression often arises in response to such a wife's ego-syntonic patterns of repeatedly rejecting his masculine position. These women deny such patterns, camouflaging a pathological attitude of narcissistic entitlement. On the other hand, the depressed husband of such a woman is apt to accept her denials and the narcissistic injuries on the basis of feelings of nonentitlement.

Many years ago, the wife of a physician was in analysis on account of a depressive neurosis. Repeatedly she had aborted, despite her intense wish for a child, attested to by sustained efforts to have physical treatment before severe depression became evident. Her childhood was marred by her mother's physical illness shortly after her birth. As the only child, she had come to be heavily involved in the care of the invalid as she grew up and had become more and more resentful before the mother's demise. It turned out that, as might have been expected, she was loaded with guilt concerning her mother and her care of her which, before analysis, was largely dissociated. In the analysis, it became evident to her that she did not feel entitled to have a child. The adverse dyadic childhood situation had adversely affected, one might say infected, the course of the succeeding triadic phase of her development, as also might have been expected; and it was only in the unraveling of the complexities of the oedipal phase of her childhood, associated with the intensification of both wish-fantasies and expectations of punishment, that the depressive symptoms began to yield in the analysis. Later in the analysis she sustained a pregnancy and had a baby. It is my impression that many cases of childlessness have a similar psychosomatic basis, that is, a deep-seated notion and feeling of nonentitlement. Often this is heavily defended against consciously and disavowed.

In his essay "Some Character Types Met With in Psychoanalytic Work," Freud (1916) discusses those wrecked by success. He takes as one example Shakespeare's Lady Macbeth, "who collapses on reaching success, after striving for it with single-minded energy" (31) ruthlessly contesting the scruples of her ambitious yet at first too tender-minded husband. Freud states: "I believe that Lady Macbeth's illness, the transformation of her callousness into penitence, could be explained directly as a reaction to her childlessness, by which she is convinced of her impotence against the decrees of nature, and at the same time reminded that it is through her own fault if her crime has been robbed of the better part of its fruits" (321–22). As I have just indicated by the preceding clinical vignette, the sequence is psychosomatic rather than somatopsychic, though there is, of course, a dynamic, circular system in clinical cases so that childlessness comes to confirm the deep-seated readiness for feelings of nonentitlement. In Shakespeare's play, as Freud points out, there is no time for a long, drawn-out disappointment of hopes for offspring to break the woman down and drive the man to defiant rage, but there is an insistent theme of childlessness representing ultimate failure.

Freud next turns to discuss Rebecca (Gamvick) West of Ibsen's *Rosmersholm* as another example of those wrecked by success. Rebecca is the femme fatale par excellence, all the more dangerous because she appears in the disguise of the inspiring muse. In *Rosmersholm*, as is typical for Ibsen, we are at first confronted with a seemingly bland situation, but as the drama unfolds we are led to discover complex relationships, and sinister secrets are revealed. Ibsen himself, in a letter which portrays *Rosmersholm* as a modern psychomachy with clashing faculties within each of the minds of the protagonists, summarizes some of the disclosures:

> the play also deals with the struggle which all serious-minded human beings have to wage with themselves in order to bring their lives into harmony with their convictions.
>
> For the different spiritual functions do not develop evenly and abreast of each other in any one human being. The acquisitive instinct hurries on from gain to gain. The moral consciousness—what we call conscience—is, on the other hand, very conservative. It has its roots deep in traditions and in the past generally. Hence the conflict within the individual. [Sprinchorn 1964, 265]

All this, and more, appeared in *Rosmersholm* in 1886, seven years before the joint publication of a "Preliminary Communication" by Breuer and Freud. Little wonder that *Rosmersholm*, of all Ibsen's plays the most inexhaustible, fascinated Freud.

In his essay, Freud focuses attention on Rebecca, the adopted daughter of Dr. West, who brought her up to be a freethinker and to despise the restrictions that the Christian religion imposes on the sensual joys of life. Following the death of Dr. West, she schemes to find a position as resident companion to the invalid wife of John Rosmer. Rosmersholm has been the stately manor for many generations of a venerable family whose members know nothing of laughter and cultivate a lofty dignity, sacrificing joy to a rigid fulfillment of duty to the community. Around the walls of the living room hang portraits, both old and more recent, of clergymen, military officers, and public officials. The present occupants are John Rosmer, a former pastor, and his sick wife, the childless Beata. Rebecca becomes infatuated with the highborn Rosmer and resolves to remove the wife from her path, making use of her fearless free will, restrained by no scruples. She contrives for Beata to read a medical book which affirms the central purpose of marriage to be the begetting of children. The wretched Beata soon begins to doubt whether she is entitled to be the wife of John Rosmer. Rebecca then hints that Rosmer, with whom she is involved in studies and exchanges of ideas, is becoming ready to abandon his old faith and join the progressive political "party of enlightenment" then active in the nearby small town. Rebecca ruthlessly proceeds to communicate to Beata that she will soon have to leave; the implication is of the need to conceal the consequences of illicit intercourse with Rosmer. All of this is totally in the realm of lies and deceit. The chronic mental sickness of Beata is thus finally worsened to the point that she throws herself from the path beside the mill into the millrace, possessed by the sense of her own worthlessness and wishing no longer to stand between her beloved husband and his happiness.

The action proceeds to show that Rebecca cannot avail herself of the success of her plot. She comes to feel that "nonentitlement" of which Kriegman writes, and she cannot accept John Rosmer's offers of marriage. Beata's presence persists wraithlike in the house, and there is the repeated sighting of the night-riding white horses that, by local legend, appear to foretell imminent death in the household. The final relationship between John Rosmer and Rebecca West is strangely compelling and issues in double suicide when they both surrender to the destructive energies of the mill-race, as Beata had surrendered before them.

Freud (1916) elucidates from a careful study of the text of Ibsen's tragic drama that behind the more evident "multiple motivation" there is a partially concealed motive, namely, the final evocation of Rebecca's previously dissociated feelings of guilt in the reproach of actual incest. He writes: "The enigma of Rebecca's behavior is susceptible of only one solution. The news that Dr. West was her father is the heaviest blow that can befall her, for she was not only his adopted daughter but had been his mistress. When Kroll began to speak, she thought he was hinting at these [illicit] relations, the truth of which she would probably have admitted and justified by her emancipated ideas. But this was far from the Rector's intention; he knew nothing of the love-affair with Dr. West, just as she knew nothing of Dr. West's being her father" (328).

And Freud writes finally in regard to such women wrecked by such success: "The practicing psycho-analytic physician knows how frequently, or how invariably, a girl who enters a household as servant, companion or governess, will consciously or unconsciously weave a day-dream, which derives from the Oedipus complex, of the mistress of the house disappearing and the master taking the newcomer as his wife in her place. *Rosmersholm* is the greatest work of art of the class that treats of this common phantasy in girls. What makes it into a tragic drama is the extra circumstance that the heroine's day-dream had been preceded in

85

her childhood by a precisely corresponding reality" (330–31). It is evident that in 1916 when this essay was written the traumatic power of sexual seduction and breach of the incest taboo remained heeded in the structure of Freud's thought, however much emphasis he had come to give to the unconscious fantasy of the inner world.

Certainly in this as in his other plays, Ibsen's personal traumatic experiences (and his early life had more than a fair share of these) are represented together with his inner world of fantasy. For example, in *Rosmersholm* the minor character Peter Mortensgaard, the editor of the liberal and progressive *Beacon* newspaper, is an obvious decomposition product of unfinished business in Ibsen's own ego. In a drama, as in a dream, split-up parts of the ego may be represented, and in the case of the calculating, liberal Mortensgaard this is starkly evident. He is depicted as a man with a "tainted past," fired from his teaching post for "moral turpitude." It turns out that he had had a child by an older woman and "had to pay the price." When Ibsen was a seventeen-year-old apothecary's apprentice, a woman ten years older than Ibsen, one of two servants in the house of his master at Grimstadt, became pregnant and returned to her parents' home to bear him a son. Out of his small salary, young Ibsen had to pay paternity costs toward the boy's upbringing until he reached the age of fourteen. In *Rosmersholm* not only the patrician conservative Kroll but Mrs. Helseth, the humble housekeeper, consider Mortensgaard as nonentitled to leadership on account of his past guilt. It is not my purpose here to pursue the influence of Ibsen's experience in life upon his imagination. He himself characterized his works as "self-anatomies," and his plays reflect his observations and experience and his inner world of fantasy based on these. His was a very divided soul, and he suffered throughout his life from severe inner conflicts. He sought to find relief from, to understand, and to work out his own conflicts through his art when developing the dramatic conflicts portrayed in his plays.

"Nonentitlement" and Ibsen

Before the advent of Rebecca's feelings of nonentitlement, that is, before her defenses crumbled, she showed considerable chutzpah—she seemed to think that she was entitled to exceptional privileges. Thus in Act II:

Rebecca: John!
Rosmer (turns): What! Were you in my bedroom? What were you doing in there?
Rebecca: (going over to him): I was listening.
Rosmer: No, but Rebecca—how could you!
Rebecca: Why shouldn't I? He was so snide—about my dressing gown.
Rosmer: Ah, so you were listening too, why Kroll—?
Rebecca: Yes, I wanted to hear what his scheme was.
Rosmer: I would have told you.
Rebecca: You wouldn't have told me quite everything. And certainly not in his words.
Rosmer: Then you heard it all?
Rebecca: Just about, I think. I had to go downstairs a moment when Mortensgaard came.
Rosmer: And then back up again.
Rebecca: John dear, don't be annoyed.
Rosmer: You do whatever you think right and proper. You have full freedom of action—But what about all this, Rebecca—? Oh I don't think I've ever needed you so much as now.

This excerpt might indicate the degree to which John Rosmer came under Rebecca's superordinate ascendancy and control. Later, in contrast, she acknowledges her own subjugation by him and the Rosmersholm tradition he embodies. Ibsen had become interested in hypnosis at this time. Indeed, a couple of years after *Rosmersholm* his ambivalent Scandinavian coeval, August Strindberg, took up the theme energetically with terrifying effect in *Creditors*. But Rebecca's psychological ascendancy, well nigh hypnotic in its effect on John Rosmer, becomes progressively undermined in the play in the subtle transactional processes represented in the sequential dialogues between Rebecca and Rosmer and Rebecca and Kroll.

Meyer (1971) recounts that a woman admirer waylaid Ibsen in the Maximilian Strasse, Munich, one day in 1889, accompanied him to his apartment, and spent an hour with him, which she found "very interesting" but rather upsetting. He spoke about hypnosis and the power of the will. She recalled: "He underlined that women's will in particular tends to remain undeveloped; we dream and wait for something unknown that will give our lives meaning. As a result of this women's emotional lives are unhealthy, and they fall victims to disappointment." At the time it would seem that Ibsen was especially preoccupied with the play he was about to write, *Hedda Gabler*. Of course, there are women like this and some men, just as he declaimed. In his time, as in ours, there were many women who did fit the description. Ibsen was assailed mercilessly by the misogynist Strindberg for being a champion of feminism because he believed that the oppression of women in society resulted in their development becoming stultified and that this should be remedied by political action.

The transactions between Rebecca and Rosmer are illuminated by every word and sentence and every gesture and movement with masterful economy in the play. We soon realize that they represent profoundly regressive, unconscious resonances, including a strong current of mutual identification and a pooling of unconscious fantasies. These become hypercathected with eventual domination of their joint archaic superego and the issue in their suicide together. The erotic undercurrent is by contrast never acted out and is finally repressed. In this context I wish to draw attention to the fate of feelings of exaggerated entitlement as they become those of nonentitlement.

At first willful and antipathetic to the crippling traditions of Rosmersholm, Rebecca rationalizes her defiance in her joint endeavors with John Rosmer in a projected mission of ennobling mankind. She does not appear altogether without conscience, for even in the "soul-murder," as Strindberg (see Meyer 1971, 564) designated her crime against Beata, she sees herself driven most of the way by a rescue fantasy, that is, to deliver John Rosmer from stagnation in marital misery to creativity in which she is the muse. At first, all of her qualms are still, and those of Rosmer stilled by her, from which we infer a dissociative defense of the archaic core of her own superego. This dissociation, supported by denials, minimizations, and rationalizations, is gradually breached as those supportive defenses are attenuated in the drawing near of the completion of her nefarious scheme; and then in the moment of success she feels utterly nonentitled to marriage with John Rosmer. This dissolution of the repertoire of her defenses comes about as her wishes for success become more and more highly charged when she nears success. The confrontations with Kroll follow, after which the severe regression in the superego becomes evident. Then she is bound to identify with the drowned Beata, whom they both join in the millrace.

Ibsen often deals in his plays with wounded and sick people and, for this reason, was dubbed by Jelliffe and Brink (1919) as the apostle of psychopaths. It is evident that these characters are not depicted as guilt-free in the depths of their psyches. But what of the wretched Beata? As Rebecca said, "She'd gotten it into her head that a childless wife had no right to be here. And then she convinced herself that her duty was to step aside for somebody else." In the play and counterplay of the players Ibsen consistently shows the unconscious group interaction; in the case of Beata she found her major counterplayer in Rebecca, who was driven to reinforce her feelings of nonentitlement to survive. Beata could not, as we say, justify her existence any longer.

As in so-called survivor guilt following destruction of companions, some people adversely compare their value to that of others. It does not require catastrophic stress for others to feel similarly though often less intensely. The very thought of having to justify one's existence is already expressive of a doubt about the right to be in the world, to be entitled to live.

We all know of the enormous impact of the early mother-child relation on the fate of the individual. Love is a *tremendum* in the primary unit. The confidence to have a child is based on the earlier confidence established when a child, and when this confidence is shaken, as in the case of Ibsen's Beata, and in the case of the patient in analysis who had difficulties maintaining a pregnancy, the resulting childlessness is looked upon as a confirmation of inner unworthiness.

When I was dealing with the patient with depressive neurosis after her experience of repeated spontaneous abortions, I became familiar with the work of Therese Benedek (1956). Thirty years ago she wrote about the dynamic circular processes within the primary unit of mother and child. She insisted that the feeling of confidence is originally an intrapsychic precipitate of positive libidinal processes in the early symbiotic phase. On the other hand, she discussed the transactional processes of ambivalent relationships between mothers and their children that predisposed individuals to depressive and psychosomatic disorders in later life by reducing the stability of confidence and of hope. The balance between the positive (libidinal, gratifying) and the negative (hostile, frustrating) symbiotic events influences the ego organization of both the child and the mother, including in the latter the developmental integration of motherliness.

Of course, the development of confidence in the child not only depends on the mother's capacity to give but also on the child's innate ability to receive, to suck, to assimilate, and to thrive. If the infant, because of congenital or acquired disability, cannot be satisfied, he or she remains frustrated and, in time, frustrates the mother. The frustration of the mother manifests itself in anger and discouragement, in fear of incompetence and in guilt and feelings of nonentitlement. These attitudes and feelings affect the further course of the emotional symbiosis. Obviously this course can become that of a vicious cycle instead of the benignly favorable cycle engendered by a loving mother and a thriving infant.

Ibsen's dramatic characters display the superstructures built upon a fragile ego fundament. In particular, the early disturbed pairing of mother and child is reflected in the later attempted pairing of Rebecca West and John Rosmersholm, whose initially mutually nourishing relationship becomes disturbed and enters a vicious cycle which includes oedipal guilt and remorse, as Freud pointed out.

There is a focus in many of Ibsen's plays on the theme of the death of the child and its reverberations, and the same theme is in the background in some of his other plays, as d'Heurle and Feimer (1976) have worked out in some detail. Thus in *Little Eyolf*, the logic of the drama requires the death of Eyolf so that Rita and Alfred can continue their ruthless unveiling of deceptions and ready themselves for the responsibility that is required for bringing up children "who do not fear life," who in Kriegman's terms feel quite entitled to live and enjoy and who are ready to meet the tasks presented at every phase of the human life cycle.

Rebecca West is, of course, a creation of Ibsen's fertile imagination, but she is representative of many childless women who nowadays come to the professional notice of psychiatrists and psychoanalysts and who oscillate between feelings of exaggerated entitlement and those of nonentitlement, in phases of defensive self-exaltation and impaired self-esteem.

REFERENCES

Benedek, T. 1956. Towards the biology of the depressive constellation. *J. Am. Psychoanal. Assn.* 4:389–427.

d'Heurle, A., and J. Feimer. 1976. Lost children: The role of the child in the psychological plays of Henrik Ibsen. *Psychoanal. Rev.* 63:27–47.

Freud, S. 1916. Some character types met with in psychoanalytic work. In *Standard edition*, 14:311–33. London: Hogarth Press, 1957.

Jelliffe, S. E., and L. Brink. 1919. *Psychoanal. Rev.* 6:357–78.

Kriegman, G. 1983. Entitlement attitudes: Psychosocial and therapeutic implications. *J. Am. Acad. Psychoanal.* 11:265–81.

Levin, S. 1969. A common type of marital incompatibility. *J. Am. Psychoanal. Assn.* 17:421–36.

Meyer, M. 1971. *Ibsen: A biography.* New York: Doubleday.

Sprinchorn, E. 1964, ed. *Ibsen: Letters and speeches.* New York: Hill and Wang.

7.

Concluding Remarks: From an Inchoate Sense of Entitlement to a Mature Attitude of Entitlement

Maurice Apprey

O NE'S SENSE OF ENTITLEMENT largely determines whether he or she will arrogantly try to claim more than his or her share of life's pleasures and benefits, often at the expense of others; fail to claim what is appropriately his or her due and suffer consequent ineffectual distress; or sturdily, and without prejudice, stride forth to meet opportunity, rejoicing in good fortune but taking disappointment without shame.

Man is, fortunately, neither an angel nor wholly a monster, and a primitive attitude of entitlement, which is not only narcissistic but often rapacious, is usually modified, at least to some degree, by the influence of civilization and can, indeed, evolve into that mature sense of entitlement that indicates a healthy zest for life with all its vicissitudes.

Although only recently viewed as a clinical construct, the sense of entitlement is implicated in practically all psychoanalytic models: drive theory, interpersonal relations, ego psychology, object relations, self-regulation, and interactional regulation. Entitlement is an issue when a child wants to own his or her body, to separate from his or her original caretakers, and to grow up to become attached to someone he or she loves and from whom he or she has expectations both tacit and expressed. What unites all these models is the sense of ownership of a human body and the way in which new representations of one's self and of others replaces the child's initial sense of body ownership. I suggest that how one's body was owned in early life affects how that ownership is delegated back to the growing individual's body-self. The mother's sanction of this recovery and ownership is crucial.

Let me illustrate a vignette from my notes on a child I observed in her home in England from the time of her birth to four years of age. I will call the child Paula and her mother Mrs. B. Mrs. B. loved caring for her infant; after bathing her, she would wrap her in a large towel and rhythmically rock her and sing to her. I enjoyed watching this routine without comment. Eighteen months later, Mrs. B. left me in charge of Paula one day while she left the room for a brief time. What did Paula do? She picked up a soft baby doll, put it on her lap, sat in front of a mirror, and rocked her baby, singing to it in a most affectionate way. When her mother returned, I drew her attention to Paula's actions and asked if they were familiar to her. She hesitated and then suddenly remembered, laughing happily. Paula grew up to be proud of her body, herself, and her achievements, and occasional reports from her mother indicate that they are both thriving.

A note on a less fortunate child, a two-and-a-half-year-old boy in a nursery, is also to the point. David was playing outside with a group of children, from time to time leaving his playmates to pick up candy that did not belong to him and putting it in his little sack. After playing again for a few minutes, he would return to the candy, only then taking it from his sack to eat. He did this three times; it was as though he acknowledged that he had no right to the candy and needed time to repress the mode of his acquisition, or to divert his little superego, before he could convince himself that the candy was rightfully his.

Those treating adolescents cannot fail to be aware of their struggle to own and master their own bodies and how this struggle can become globalized in ways that impede mastery of learning, of a sense of autonomy, of an appropriate sense of entitlement: these are impediments that hamper the adolescent's ultimate attainment of sexual organization. Direct observation, clinical constructions, transference phenomena, and other clinical manifestations persuade us that there are antecedents to the acquisition of a mature person's sense of entitlement. The chapters in this book, all reflecting the vicissitudes of the sense of entitlement, motivated me to articulate a developmental line from an inchoate, instinct-ridden sense of entitlement to a mature and acquired attitude of entitlement. The concept of developmental lines (Anna Freud 1965) is valuable in diagnostic work and in metapsychological formulation in general. She originally put forward six developmental lines, the prototype of which was the line from "emotional dependency to emotional self-reliance and adult object relationships" (64). Her work on developmental lines helps alert psychoanalytic practitioners and diagnosticians to imbalances and developmental disharmonies that cause friction between innate and environmental factors. The previous chapters provide the five way stations in the line of development from inchoate to mature entitlement that I posit.

1. An inchoate, instinct-ridden sense of entitlement fueled by a constellation of preoedipal issues that include the negotiation of

inside and outside, self and other(s), me and not-me, mine and not-mine. These negotiations are governed by the immaturity of the child's ego, his egocentricity, his relative proneness to primary process thinking, and the peremptoriness of his wishes that influences his evaluation of time. Because he is immature, envy, grandiosity, and other narcissistic attitudes may determine the ways in which he asserts entitlement. Along with these negotiations, the sense of having one's body-self appropriately owned shifts to the sense of owning it oneself, thus permitting the mother's narcissism and sense of entitlement to be passed on to the child.

2. From the infantile entitlement wishes of the preoedipal period comes a period when the now oedipal child negotiates entitlement wishes, transforming parricidal impulses into identification with admired objects. Hitherto solipsistic entitlement wishes that led the individual to fantasize unlimited possibilities are narrowed down to a negotiation of "Who should be excluded to gain primacy with whom?"

3. A postoedipal expansion of an object-related sense of entitlement in which the child recognizes that: "I count, you count; I matter, you matter." Appropriate reaction formations and the emergence of sublimation potential brings the repression of the instinctual sense of entitlement and concomitant humility. Now the sense of entitlement begins to regulate self-esteem less and less uncertainly.

4. A mature sense of identity that withstood the instinctual eruption of puberty and early adolescence; a maturity that enables the child to accept an increasingly realistic view of parents and to handle the shift from familial to extrafamilial ties. There then comes a sense of entitlement evident in the relative constancy of the self and object representation with minimum fluctuation.

5. A mature sense of entitlement that allows the young person to give up the discrepancy between expressed entitlement and felt nonentitlement. Now the sense of entitlement is acquiescent, ac-

cepts reality, and moves away from gross narcissism and the related rejection of one's existential situation of utter finiteness. Entitlement can now accommodate an external reality of accepting one's self as one really is and the world for what it is. Within this sense of entitlement one can maneuver one's own self and others to expand one's options. The development of a sense of entitlement that allows maximization of one's options and the concurrent reduction of adverse consequences opens the way for hope and fulfillment.

A successful negotiation of these way stations can provide a firm platform for adulthood. The maturity that comes with aging can only add to the continuous psychic restructuring that comes with the acquisition of a mature sense of entitlement and the freedom to forfeit that sense of entitlement as when, for instance, there is the fear of one's own impending death or that of a close family member. Over the course of the five way stations in the developmental line to a mature and acquired sense of entitlement, archaic regulatory factors have gradually been supplanted by relatively effective ego regulations. I echo Hartmann's (1958) notion of "change of function" (49) that articulates the process whereby an instinctual ego gradually becomes subordinate to a mature autonomous one, and I further suggest that all other developmental lines follow this change of function.

References

Freud, A. 1965. *The writings of Anna Freud*. Vol. 6: *Normality and pathology in childhood: Assessments of development*. New York: International Universities Press.

Hartmann, H. 1958. *Ego psychology and the problem of adaptation*. New York: International Universities Press.

Contributors

Name Index

Subject Index

Contributors

D. WILFRED ABSE, M.D., is Professor Emeritus (psychiatry), University of Virginia. He is also a practicing psychoanalyst and consulting psychiatrist at St. Albans Hospital in Radford, Virginia.

MAURICE APPREY is Associate Professor of Psychiatry, Department of Behavioral Medicine and Psychiatry, and Assistant Dean, Student Affairs, School of Medicine, University of Virginia, Charlottesville.

CECIL C. H. CULLANDER, M.D., is a practicing psychoanalyst in Charlottesville, Virginia, and Clinical Professor of Psychiatry, Department of Behavioral Medicine and Psychiatry, University of Virginia, Charlottesville.

ROBERT M. DORN, M.D., was Professor of Psychiatry and Chief of Child, Adolescent and Family Psychiatry, Department of Psychiatry, University of California at Davis. Currently, he is a Clinical Professor in the Department of Psychiatry at Davis and a practicing psychoanalyst.

GEORGE KRIEGMAN, M.D., was the first president of the Virginia Psychoanalytic Society and practiced psychoanalysis in Richmond. He served as Clinical Professor at the Medical College of Virginia, Richmond.

ROBERT MICHELS, M.D., is Professor and Chairman, Department of Psychiatry, Cornell University, New York, New York, and Training and Supervising Analyst, Columbia Psychoanalytic Institute, New York.

TERRY C. RODGERS, M.D., was formerly a practicing psycho-analyst in Norfolk, Virginia, and Professor of Clinical Psychiatry, Department of Psychiatry and Behavioral Sciences, Eastern Virginia Medical School, Norfolk. Presently, Dr. Rodgers resides in Rancho Santa Fe, California.

MICHEL SILBERFELD, M.D., is Staff Psychiatrist and Head, Division of Psychological Medicine, the Princess Margaret Hospital, Department of Medical Oncology; Staff Psychiatrist and Director, Psychiatric Emergency Services, the Wellesley Hospital; Assistant Professor of Psychiatry, Preventive Medicine, University of Toronto, Toronto, Ontario.

VAMIK D. VOLKAN, M.D., is Professor of Psychiatry and Director of the Division of Psychoanalytic Studies, Department of Behavioral Medicine and Psychiatry, University of Virginia, Charlottesville. He is Medical Director of Blue Ridge Hospital, a division of the University of Virginia Medical Center, Charlottesville, and is Training and Supervising Analyst at the Washington Psychoanalytic Institute, Washington, D.C.

Name Index

Subject Index